PEDAGOGY OF GLOBAL EVENTS

Pedagogy of Global Events explores a relatively new phenomenon of cultural events—concerts, media experiences, and film series—designed to bring attention to global problems and spark action. This case-based analysis addresses a range of events to consider questions about what it means to educate the wider public about significant global challenges, the meaning and limits of these efforts, and how media refracts these experiences. The analyses are informed by data collected from organizers of special events, participants in attendance, those viewing online or after-the-fact through media representations, as well as through a careful analysis of web artifacts created by and in response to the events. By offering rare empirical analyses of global events, this book is valuable reading for organizers and attendees alike.

Timothy J. Patterson is Assistant Professor of Social Studies Education at Temple University, Philadelphia, USA.

William Gaudelli is Dean of Education and Vice Provost for Innovation in Education at Lehigh University, Bethlehem, USA.

PEDAGOGY OF GLOBAL EVENTS

Insights from Concerts, Film Festivals and Social Network Happenings

Timothy J. Patterson and William Gaudelli

Routledge
Taylor & Francis Group

NEW YORK AND LONDON

Designed cover image: Atit Phetmuangtong / EyeEm / Getty Images

First published 2023
by Routledge
605 Third Avenue, New York, NY 10158

and by Routledge
4 Park Square, Milton Park, Abingdon, Oxon, OX14 4RN

Routledge is an imprint of the Taylor & Francis Group, an informa business

Library of Congress Cataloging-in-Publication Data
Names: Patterson, Timothy J. (Educator), author. |
Gaudelli, William, author.
Title: Pedagogy of global events : insights from concerts, film festivals
and social network happenings / Timothy J. Patterson, William Gaudelli.
Description: New York : Routledge, 2023. | Includes bibliographical
references and index.
Identifiers: LCCN 2022041077 | ISBN 9780367242824 (Hardcover) |
ISBN 9780367242848 (Paperback) | ISBN 9780429281570 (eBook)
Subjects: LCSH: Special events--Management--Case studies. |
Mass media--Audiences. | Education and globalization. | Critical pedagogy.
Classification: LCC GT3405 .P38 2023 | DDC 394.2068--dc23/eng/20221205
LC record available at https://lccn.loc.gov/2022041077

ISBN: 978-0-367-24282-4 (hbk)
ISBN: 978-0-367-24284-8 (pbk)
ISBN: 978-0-429-28157-0 (ebk)

DOI: 10.4324/9780429281570

Typeset in Bembo
by SPi Technologies India Pvt Ltd (Straive)

CONTENTS

ACKNOWLEDGMENTS

Timothy would like to thank the following research assistants at Temple University for their diligent and detailed support of this project: Laurie Esposito, Andrea Terrero Gabbadon, Amani Rush, and Valerie Woxholdt. Dr. Michael Levine at Wichita State University was a constant sounding board for ideas on researching concerts and social network events, and provided many helpful pathways for documenting the history of global concerts. Finally, this book would not be possible without the continuous love and support of Timothy's wife Kathleen and his children Ella and Malcolm. Much gratitude is owed to the three of them for providing him the time and space to conduct this research.

William would like to thank research assistants at Lehigh University including Yael Gross and Marsha Ariol for their support throughout the project along with Becky Ford of Teachers College, Columbia University. William also is forever grateful for the love and support of his family, Liz and Alex.

Finally, we offer our sincerest appreciation for the support of our editors at Routledge: Catherine Bernard who advocated for this book when it was just an idea and Matthew Friberg who patiently guided us through the writing process, as well as editorial assistants Mari Zajac and Jessica Cooke.

1

INTRODUCTION

Global Events and Public Pedagogy

Pedagogy of Global Events (PGE) examines the use of spectacle events, such as concerts, in terms of their educational purpose and value. What does it mean to have a concert to address an issue such as famine, or for people ravaged by political violence, or to promote a framework for sustainable development? What is learned in these events, by whom, and to what ends? These are the questions that were swimming in our heads in the decade that preceded the development of this book. As educators—and as educators who prepare teachers to engage social issues from a global perspective—we were drawn to understanding what these events mean in the moments that they are enacted and how they are understood by participants in the midst of the spectacle and in the afterglow of having attended the events. Did they matter? Were they informative? In what ways? And how did these events serve a broader purpose of galvanizing solidarity for causes, issues, or problems that, lacking a spectacle or a concert, would garner less attention and therefore less resolve to address the concern?

This chapter explores the overarching themes of the book, or the interaction of learning, events, and global issues. We look first to scholarship that grounds these efforts, specifically media reception studies, public pedagogy, and lastly, global citizenship education (GCE). Each of these discourses is consequential to the current study though in different, complementary ways. Media reception studies will focus on how audiences perceive media objects and what meanings they draw along with the rapidly changing landscape, expanding media outlets, and ubiquitous access.

An important piece of *PGE* is the events themselves and the uses of media—defined broadly as performing artists, social media, films/documentaries, and texts—that are deployed therein. We will then turn to the pedagogical issues, specifically, conceptions of public pedagogy along with affective/motivational

DOI: 10.4324/9780429281570-1

forms of education. This will sharpen the focus on the experiences of participants and how they form meanings from the events and the degree to which they are inspired to engage in action. Lastly, we will examine some of the literature on GCE as a way of framing the contents of the events. GCE, in part, draws from a recognition of the significant global challenges—poverty, hunger, global warming—that the current nation-based system is ill-designed to address along with the requisite need to educate young people, and indeed all people, about taking actions to address them.

Media Reception

Media is increasingly pervasive in daily life. The expansion of screen-time through cells and other handheld devices coupled with an immediacy that constantly demands and draws attention have created an all-encompassing ecosystem of media. As the Pew Charitable Trusts (2022) notes,

> Technology has changed how people consume news, as well as the process of gathering it. Information is now almost instantaneous and available anywhere in the world. And news has been democratized so that voices outside the mainstream can be heard.

Yet, the openness of media has also undermined the standing of some news organizations, particularly national news outlets, also known as legacy outlets. For instance, among registered Republicans, trust in national news declined between 2016 and 2021 from 70% to 35%, or a loss of half of the respondents in just a five-year period, along with declines among Democrats (−3%) and independents (−17%) over that same time period. While access to creating stories and disseminating "news" has clearly increased, there is now widespread distrust of some media, particularly legacy media outlets (e.g., *The New York Times* or *ABC News*). A further illustration of this dynamic change is that the number of adults ages 18–29 who report receiving TV via cable or satellite at home is down since 2015 from 65% to 34% (Pew Charitable Trusts, 2022). These studies demonstrate a significant shift in how young people are receiving media along with what sense people are making of the media they are consuming and subsequently the trust that they have in what is being received.

Distrust of legacy or mainstream media, particularly around explicitly political messages, has been a consequence of the widening landscape and subsequent choices available to consumers over the past 25 years. As Müller (2021) notes, people are now more in control than ever in creating their own media ecosystem out of the "infinite," which has created an echo chamber for news and information customized to the social and political tastes of the consumer (p. 70). The wide distribution of media affords significant agency to the consumer to choose what information they consume and when, allowing busy people to fit media consumption into everyday life. Too, the speed of information availability provides consumers with access 24/7/365 rather than having to wait for the daily news cycle of a bygone era. This intensification, coupled with the penetrative capacity of bespoke, personalized media that really "fits" the consumer, affirms their identity through affinity groups. Thus, as people fill their ecosystem through social media platforms with those ideas, narratives, symbols, images, and grammars that resonate with an identity, there is a level of enmeshment such that the distinction between self and mediated self begins to dissolve.

Scholarship in media studies, and reception studies in particular, can be traced to the widespread adoption of television in the mid-twentieth century, coupled with the work of leading scholars such as Stuart Hall, Roland Barthes, and Umberto Eco, among others. Much of this discourse is situated around the nexus of viewer and media, on the interplay between how people view media, understand its meanings, decode its symbols, and interpret its meaning individually and socially. Schrøder (2000) provides an elegant summary of continua of interpretation and the limits of these frames of thinking about media reception. Hall's first continuum of encoding–decoding includes poles of *dominant* and *oppositional* with a center point of *negotiated*. Thus, the dominant read of media is an adoption of the encoded meaning that is intended by the author, or a taking at face value the media's message about a situation or social scene. *Law and Order*, for example, the long-running television serial, encodes messages about a violent New York City tamed ultimately by a fair, if imperfect, criminal justice and judicial system. Thus, a *dominant* reading of this serial is to accept and affirm this perspective as "true" or "given." An *oppositional* reading, however, would be to decode *Law and Order* as offering a white, middle-class perspective about police work in New York City, one that occludes the systemic racism inherent in the criminal justice and justice systems of urban centers in the US. And in Hall's framing, a *negotiated* stance is one that accepts some aspects of the encoded/intended media message and refracts elements of that message to qualify, through personal experience or otherwise, the messages as an act of decoding.

The second axis of media reception studies is the polysemic and monosemic continuum (Schrøder, 2000). The monosemic text is one where the encoded meaning is *the* meaning of the text while a polysemic text is one that creates multiple and polyphonous perspectives, not singularized into *what the media means*. Schrøder (2000) enjoins the debate about the usefulness of these heuristics, begging the questions, "Is there a 'preferred reading'? How may it be defined? How can we know it? And how great is its power to constrain audience readings?" The last question is perhaps the most significant of all, as it calls into question the extent to which media can have volition to "enter people's consciousness" directly and without refraction, or put oppositely, the agency of a viewer to block ideas or narratives encoded within a text for circumspection and interrogation. Schrøder argues that these devices, while useful, are unable to capture the ranges of responses that people actually give to media, through her and colleagues' experiences in focus groups and interviews. She argues for a more dynamic, multidimensional model, one that analyzes text (media), motivation, comprehension, position, and discrimination (or, the ability to discern messages and read between and underneath a text) (p. 243). Regardless of how one tries to frame and theorize the reception of media, plasticity inheres within media, and thus limits the ability of an explanatory theory to capture the scrum that arises from most media texts. Mathieu (2015) summarizes Hall's analysis accordingly:

> Hall's work initiated and still to date encapsulates important orientations for the relevance of reception analysis: 1) that meaning is an essential question in media studies, 2) that it must be studied not only in the text (encoding), but also in context (or its decoding), 3) that the investigation should understand the interplay between text and context.
>
> *(pp. 17–18)*

Mathieu (2015) poses a new set of interactive spaces that have been created—and deserve scholarly attention—with the advent of social media. These nexus points include: (1) the introduction of media texts into social media, positioning the user-audience as a gatekeeper, (2) the insertion of the audience-user into the media text, often through the deployment of irony and oppositional memes, such that positionality of the user is unmistakable through the text, and (3) the engagement, or spreadability, of those texts in circulation such that they rise in prominence and visibility by virtue of other audience-users on the social network (p. 30).

How one behaves as a result of viewing media has been a long-standing debate within the academic community, one that periodically spills into the public sphere. Staiger (2005) describes the early days of film and the wide-ranging debate about whether films were educative and could be used to attain certain social learning or if they were a hot-bed of violence and depravity on display that led to a more violent and licentious society (pp. 21–27). Film-makers and social scientists tested media reception in a variety of circumstances, with the results around the ultimate question—*Do films make people act differently?*—being largely inconclusive. After the rise of Marxism in Russia and elsewhere, scholars of the Frankfurt school began to introduce the concept of power into media reception analysis. Their theory generally held that the force of social assumption embedded within media, about how people live in a capitalist society, were so deeply encoded as to thwart any meaningful effort to remove them from one's viewing, such that passive viewing was the only possibility within an ideologically straight-jacketed community that was unable to escape the commodification that the film, and they, were inherently bound up within.

A rearward view of the past quarter century might suggest a few breakpoints from which this contemporary scene was spawned, particularly related to the agency of readers and their engagement in meaning-making from diverse media texts.

Perhaps most interesting is Oprah Winfrey's Book Club (OWBC), a segment on her television beginning in 1996, and its role in fueling a reading revolution that women of color coordinated and produced. The mission statement of the OWBC project clearly states their intentions: "to use television to transform people's lives, to make viewers see themselves differently and to bring happiness and a sense of fulfillment into every home" (Rooney, 2008, p. 13). OWBC brought diverse narratives into the public sphere in a way that was far more than entertainment alone but was revolutionary, both in substance and format, as the voices and issues represented a wider array of perspectives than traditional, legacy media offered and the format of what was essentially an "online book club" spawned a doubling of book clubs in the US, from approximately 250,000 prior to OWBC to 500,000 thereafter (Rooney, 2008, p. 14). This shift signaled an asset of emerging, interactive media: the ability for narratives, information, and voices previously behind the paywall of universities to reach a wider audience. Too, OWBC allowed for a sense of interactivity—if not the full-blown expression of social media—such that people felt they were engaged with the same conversation going on in their TV. Again, programs like these underscored the decoding and polysemic ways of understanding how people view media texts. OWBC also helped to flip the revenue model such that media could drive the sale of books, such that authors and publishers who landed a spot on OWBC were guaranteed a sales bump that was unimaginable in the cloistered realm of academe.

A more recent example of the flipped-media phenomenon and social affiliation modality of media is the online book club dedicated to Black women writers, called *Well-Read Black Girl* (WRBG). WRBG has a stated goal not unlike OWBC: "Our goal is to introduce a cohort of diverse writers to future generations—contemporary authors who are non-binary, queer, trans, and disabled. To address inequalities and improve communities through reading and reflecting on the works of Black women" (Wellreadblackgirl.com, n.d.). Founded by Glory Edim, WRBG focused on Black voices in literature from luminaries such as Rita Dove, Alice Walker, and Toni Morrison. The community is in some ways an updated version of OWBC in that it is a book club, but no longer through the singular mode of television and text, but a community engaged through the online space, social media, festivals, and periodic events. As theorized by Gitelman (2014), these gatherings are forms of counter-institutions, or "loosely self-organizing assemblages—of members, mail, media, and lore—that defy institutionalization partly by reproducing it cacophonously" (p. 149). The creation of these start-up-type counter-institutions deploy modalities of media divergently while drawing liberally on the content of academe to fuel the shift in aperture, the change in perceived audience. As such, these efforts draw deeply from the counter-valent tendencies of media put to new uses—away from passive receptivity in isolation toward active engagement in community—that have flipped the script on how we ought to conceptualize and engage media reception studies in the contemporary moment.

The events that we focus on in this book—from the Marda Loop Justice Film Festival in Calgary to the Global Citizen concerts in New York City—all share some of these same characteristics; that of being loosely self-organizing assemblages designed to illuminate global issues through a diverse set of voices toward building a community geared to act. It would diminish the valence of these events to singularize them as "film festival" or "concert," since while these may be the dominant activities, these events are actually divergent conglomerations of people, texts, symbols, signs, and moments that take on a life of their own as they are co-constructed and then quickly disintegrate into a past event, captured in video, image, social media post, and website but not to be experienced directly again. The ephemeral quality of the "global event" and arguably of many forms of emerging media has an aspect of disposal or forgetting that resides within the special moment of the event. And it is indeed one aspect of contemporary global events—in light of the various precedent events that we explore herein such as the Concert for Bangladesh (1971) or Live Aid (1986)—that the organizers intend to address by making pre/post commitments to service activities, as does the Global Citizen Concert.

As we surveyed the landscape of what to study in the context of writing a book about global events, we sought events that (1) are organized with explicit attention to global issues in framing, aiming to raise awareness and/or influence policy changes and/or spark citizen action to address an issue; (2) generate high levels of attention, if episodic, within the immediate venue and beyond, through various forms of media; and (3) have an explicitly educational purpose that augments the spectacle of high-profile performers or visual texts or films. And yet our primary purpose in doing this study and writing this book is less about the events themselves and the media that they were and were created in their wake, but rather to examine the learning that such events create, the receptivity as a form of media in light of the educational ends that sits at the foundation of these global events.

Public Pedagogy

We begin the title of this book with the term pedagogy, as it is a central concern of educators who prepare educators. What does it mean? We tend toward a broadly social conception, or one that is not tethered to institutional learning environments, such as a classroom, and look more to how events and concerts create spaces of learning with intentionality. John Dewey's thinking is instructive to us in this conceptualization. Dewey (1938) famously wrote about the social nature of all learning, believing society to be the repository of all knowledge and a pedagogical process as one of retrieval from that repository. Dewey sums this up in his reliance on "experience" as the touchstone of learning, meaning a temporally demarcated unit of being that could be anticipated, is engaged by a learner/being, and afterward, can be reflected upon toward drawing insights that can then be employed in understanding a future, germane situation. Dewey's notion of pedagogy is rooted in the principles of continuity and interaction. On continuity, the chaining of events, understood as such, coupled with the temporal sequencing toward some future use, illustrates his thinking about how learning recursively builds upon itself, gradually accumulating over time toward a matured and refined sense of the social world and its functioning. Secondly, the principle of interaction is as pertinent as continuity, since it is the interplay of "being-to-social world" that allows that progressive chain of sequences to become known.

Dewey relied heavily on a naturalistic conception of learning, as opposed to a formalistic or institutional one, since these "traditional" forms of learning inhered a coercive aspect that is contrary to the way people actually learn. People, by virtue of their innate tendency to "learn by doing," could naturally learn from being reflective about experience. An obvious illustration that Dewey employs is how young children learn to avoid dangers, such as touching a hot stove, through the experience of having proximity to that object while it is operating. These reactive learnings though are not equivalent to the reflective experience of a child doing everyday tasks around the house, such as cooking an egg, to understand the various conditions that affect the activity and its outcome, from the heat of the pan to the duration of cooking to the condition of the eggs. These activities, for Dewey, through the principles of continuity and interaction, lead one quickly and inductively out of the home, to the farm that produced the chickens, to the water and feed that supplied their nourishment, to the fertilizers used in their production, and on and on, in an imbricated chain from an egg to the whole of society. While Dewey's claim worked along the continuum of object to universal, Martin Luther King, Jr. made a very similar argument in one of his last public speeches regarding the fundamentally interdependent nature of being:

> It really boils down to this: that all life is interrelated. We are all caught in an inescapable network of mutuality, tied into a single garment of destiny. Whatever affects one directly, affects all indirectly. We are made to live together because of the interrelated structure of reality. ...before you finish eating breakfast in the morning, you've depended on more than half of the world. This is the way our universe is structured, this is its interrelated quality. We aren't going to have peace on earth until we recognize this basic fact of the interrelated structure of all reality.
>
> *(King, 1967)*

A great deal of scholarship has emerged over the past two decades around learning in space, place, and community, as if to describe a kind of null curriculum, or all the other places that researchers seek beyond schools to witness and analyze learning. Conceptually, space often occupies the metaphysical landscape where imaginaries and mental images work to construct meaning. The park near where we once worked and studied was an imagined boundary between neighborhoods, a metaphysical boundary that served as a liminal zone between two distinct areas of culture. Place, on the other hand, is typically understood in its physicality, or the material substances that constitute a particular location, with its geographic features and built structures. The same park, then, has long, sloping terraces and stairs that allow visitors to move into the place of the park, along with playgrounds for children, basketball courts, paths, and benches that are the physical ornaments that structure the park. And yet, the dualism at work here—physical and mental—has itself been critiqued as being too strongly tethered to Western epistemology and its fixation on distinction and difference. Thus, contemporary, critical theorists of geography, including Edward Soja and Henri Lefebvre, argue for an interstitial approach that synthesizes the physical and metaphysical, imagined and physical, as intertwined, or what Soja has coined Thirdspace. Thirdspace, according to Soja (1996), is the intersection of subjectivity and objectivity, real and imagined, knowable and unknown, mind and body, and official history and everyday life (p. 57). This conceptual move is an effort to dissolve or blur the sharp boundary between what is real and imagined, physical and perceptual, into a holistic understanding of how we think, know, and are within our surroundings.

The notion that contexts matter and shape what we learn and toward what ends we learn are often ignored in scholarship around teaching and learning. The place of learning, the social environments of learning, are treated as a kind of null curriculum that is ever-present and thus vanishingly recedes out of our conscious attention. Todd (2014) offers an acute conception of pedagogy that illustrates its relational and therefore contextual dimensions:

> Pedagogy, then, can be seen, in a general sense, to refer to the process through which these relational exchanges come to condition the kinds of knowledge we can have, and more importantly, the kind of being we can become (Castoriadis, 1997). As having its focus, therefore, on process and exchange, pedagogy enables us to think about how our becoming someone is necessarily transformative. That is, does not assume that we exist outside of these exchanges by virtue of our birth; instead, each one of us is engaged in a process of becoming that is relational and ongoing.
>
> *(p. 161)*

Todd argues that education must drive toward a change of self, perhaps as individualistic as mattering for one's personal transformation and, at times, toward much grander ends of transforming society and improving the world. This presents a kind of paradox that inheres within pedagogy, such that a learner is present in the same world that is in need of changing, thus embodying a tension between *how one is now* and *how one ought to be* through a transformative process of learning.

The uniqueness of our being, each of us, thus makes the contexts for learning and relationships fundamentally a mélange of interactions through community that is forever in flux due to the particularity of the people and experiences in that mix. "Thus, in this way, because each of us is unique and radically different, we exist in the context of plurality right from the beginning" (p. 164). In Todd's (2014) terms—drawing extensively from Hannah Arendt—the unique presence of a person, birthed by voice, text, and utterance into the world, creates the world anew through that presence, and thus changes, or breaks, the monotony of *what simply is* toward a possibility of what might become given their unique, novel presence. Returning to the idea of public pedagogy, then, Todd's conceptualization opens the way for a kind of fulsome knowing in and through the presence of others that depends on the presence of others and the everyday substance of our interactions, on the "local, contextual, and singular aspects of our daily work in the here and now" (p. 167) rather than in some romanticized abstraction that fetishizes individuality over relational being.

Our relationship with the world and the ways that we interact in and provide context and presence for others is part of a broad understanding of public pedagogy, which we take to mean the ways that we learn relationally through the multitude of experiential points in our daily lives. In that vernacular, Wang (2018) considers the genre of *Cantopop*, a popular musical form in Hong Kong that is closely related to the challenges of everyday life. Cantopop is a form of expression or utterance in the world, through song and lyric, that addresses a range of issues, including finding a place to live, dealing with political controversies, the experiences of immigrants, and the challenge of establishing a family in an urban culture, that in some ways are very specific to Hong Kong and in other ways, generalizable to many publics and places. While Wang details music that speaks to these issues and the artists who create and perform, the mechanism of distribution and dissemination, namely social media, is of particular interest. *Cantopop* relies upon users to share and distribute its locally derived, contextual media, thereby taking on a form of public pedagogy wherein people's lives are storied and shared and recipients come to interpret their experiences in light of those rendered in their shared social media feeds. Users identify strongly with the contents of *Cantopop* since they experience highly similar situations and thus the medium amplifies and resonates simultaneously with users, helping them learn about themselves and proximate others through the music.

Global Citizenship Education

The final foundation of our trio is global citizenship education, or GCE. GCE is a discourse, a set of related curricula, and a movement that focuses on transforming educational systems and practices that speak to the interdependent nature of a globally interconnected world. GCE represents the merger of two related fields of educational discourse, those being global education and citizenship education.

Global education, a curriculum that explores cultural diversity, human rights, international relations, and environmental issues, began largely in the global North during the second half of the twentieth century with the intention of helping students see the world beyond their immediate context while realizing the problematic nature of global issues that recognized no political boundaries. Citizenship education has arguably a much longer lineage as it can be traced to the early days of the national education systems (see Weber, 1976) as a means of creating affiliation through a national identity as well as a form of teaching the duties, responsibilities, and rights of citizens.

The contemporary period of globalization grew immensely in significance as a result of economic liberalization between states that began in the post-World War II period and in earnest by the early 1970s. The economic changes to the state, namely that companies and actors could shift capital across multiple locales and allowed for foreign direct investment in economies outside of the Soviet bloc countries, created the conditions of this vast integration, one that has grown immeasurably intricate as a result of the concomitant rise of internet-based technologies (see Friedman, 2006). What lagged amidst this flurry of capital and technological change, however, was a reckoning of how the economic changes would translate into other spheres of life, namely the political and the social. As to the former, the absence of a global political order to match the economic one—a thesis well-developed by a host of scholars such as Nancy Fraser (2009), Leif Wenar (2016), and Joseph Stiglitz (2017)—is a significant point of friction. While there have been well-documented efforts to create a global political order out of the disarray and chaos of conflicting state interests—such as the effort to establish sustainable development (Sachs, 2015) and global governance through shared juridical and political processes (see Slaughter, 2004)—the horror of Russia's invasion of Ukraine in February 2022 reminds us all, sadly, that the emergence of a new political order is far from a completed process and in many ways remains deeply contested in principle and practice. If one refrain captures the moment in which we are writing this book—*What can we do?*—the absence of a political order that overcomes state sovereignty foils global efforts to make peace, adjudicate atrocities, and sustain a global order that allows for human flourishing.

GCE is the expression of an awakening among teachers, educators, curriculum authors, and the wider public that our future must be rooted in a global reality. The state-container for education, so much a product of Western-style education that arose concomitant with the rise of states, is no longer adequate for the global society that we now inhabit nor for the aims that we have to produce a more just, equitable, and sustainable global society as a shared aim (see Roemhild & Gaudelli, 2021). GCE has been characterized as a "floating signifier" (Mannion et al., 2011), an ethical frame for teaching and learning (Bosio & Schattle, 2021), and a multiplicity of overlapping and at times contradictory discourses (Schattle, 2008). As UNESCO claims in their foundational text *Global Citizenship Education* (2014): "While these tensions vary, they all point to the fundamental question of how to promote universality (e.g. common and collective identity, interest, participation, duty), while respecting singularity (e.g. individual rights, self-improvement)" (p. 18).

At least some of these tensions surface around the ontic stance of curriculum devised under the aegis of GCE and the ongoing discussion about how to name what is happening under the widely used rubric. Pashby et al. (2020), in their own attempt to fashion a meta-analysis of these multiple and confusing streams of discourse, make an important and often-neglected observation: that the framing itself is an act of positionality and subjectivity, or that one always stands somewhere in order to begin the task of sorting out what belongs in which category. As they note (2020):

> The effect is to present as universal and inevitable an economic system organised by (racialised) capitalist markets, a political system organised by nation-states, a knowledge system organised by a single (European) rationality, and a mode of existence premised on autonomy and individualism.
>
> *(p. 146)*

Thus, they eloquently articulate an ongoing tension in even having a conversation about what GCE means, being these discussions often fail to recognize the inherent Western and Northern outlook in moves to organize the world. The confounding aspect of GCE—that portends to be about and for everyone in the world—is that it can come to sound omniscient in its universal impulses and thereby and ironically alienating for its purposes.

Figure 1.1 (Pashby et al., 2020) provides an illuminating visual representation of the cacophony of perspectives that intersect GCE as a broad umbrella discourse. They begin with nine published typologies of GCE by which they create an even wider image of these various aggregates and how scholars in the field express categorically what ideas and practices are at play in the discourse.

They organize their meta-meta-analysis around three common places of curriculum discourse, including neoliberal, liberal, and critical. One might think of these as primarily economic descriptions and yet so much more flows from this ontic position, including political arrangements and social outlooks, that they serve to capture most of what is discussed in GCE.

The neoliberal position is characterized by economic development, competition, entrepreneurial activity, and participation in the global market. The liberal position organizes around values such as ethical and moral outlook, cosmopolitanism, and soft/liberal humanism along with institutional practices to ensure a peaceable, ordered world. The critical position articulates structural problems that sit at the foundation of ongoing inequality, violence, oppression, and marginalization. One can readily imagine curriculum activities and learning encounters that map onto this mapping, such as the study abroad tour to learn about entrepreneurial practices in another society as neoliberal, a Model United

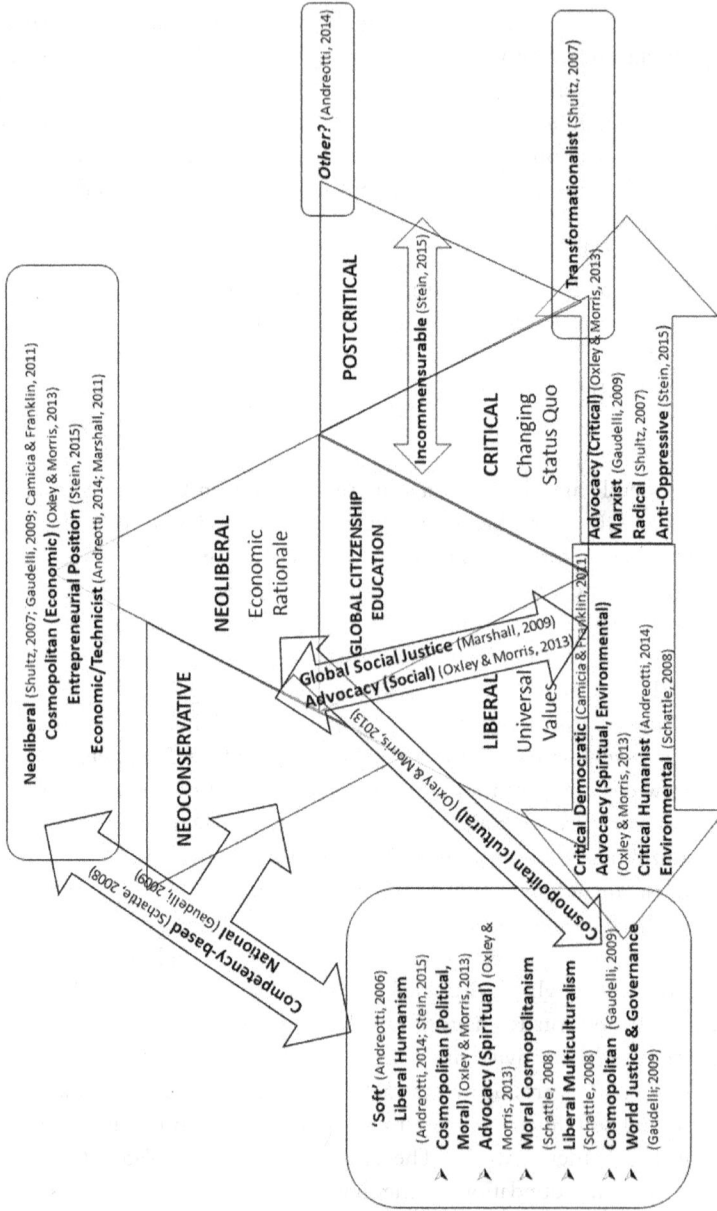

FIGURE 1.1 Interrelated Dimensions of Global Citizenship Education

Reprinted from "A Meta-Review of Typologies of Global Citizenship Education," by K. Pashby, M. da Costa, S. Stein, & V. Andreotti, 2020, *Comparative Education, 56*(2), p. 150. Used with permission.

Nations simulation as within the liberal framework, and a study of homeless-ness and gender violence as expressions of class structures and patriarchy as part of the critical domain. Pashby et al. (2020) push beyond the rigid categories, however, in seeking an interstitial, other place for GCE, attempting to imagine otherwise out of the boxology that typifies discourse and practice now. They argue that shifting away from methodological approaches to GCE—or means and modalities—toward an epistemological stance—or what things mean and how they matter to people—is a more viable path forward for the discourse. Questions that they imagine pushing GCE in that direction include:

> How can we imagine a responsibility towards others (both human and other-than-human beings), rather than a responsibility for others? What kinds of analyses can enable students to understand how they are a part of global problems, and how they can work to mitigate or eradicate these problems at a structural level (e.g. the impact of consumption levels on climate change, the role of Western military interventions in prompting migration, the racialised and gendered international division of labour, etc.)? Whose definitions of citizenship tend to dominate in GCE dis-courses, and why? How might we redefine and repurpose the concept of global citizenship to advocate for more inclusive forms of representa-tion, and the redistribution of resources? How can our ideas of global citizenship be informed not just by the national citizenship formations of Western nation-states, but also of other countries and other kinds of politi-cal communities (e.g. Indigenous nations)? How can we learn to learn from different ways of knowing in order to imagine the world differently?
>
> *(pp. 158–159)*

Their approach of recognizing the ground we currently inhabit while looking toward a horizon of possibility that might be, is generally how we view the state of GCE, and indeed, the global, public effort to educate about world problems. A lot of "water under the bridge" has transpired in the past three decades around what it means to educate society for a globally interdependent world, and at the risk of being reductionist, it may all come down to this: How can we help oth-ers to see the connectedness of their lives on this planet and what that can mean for how they act accordingly? If that question is taken seriously and in the many directions that flow from it, we believe that this current effort that we undertake to study—the global event—has transformative power in the social life of our world, one among many educational spaces that deserve our attention and energy.

What Lies Ahead

These three frames—media reception, public pedagogy, and GCE—are among the discourses that ground the study and what we make of global events. This brief introduction sets the stage for the remainder of the book and will be brought back into the discussion and extended upon at key points. Before moving too quickly from this foundation, however, we will spend a bit of space exploring why we undertook this work and how it connects to who we are and what we do. At the time of writing, I (Tim) am a researcher and practitioner of teacher education in Philadelphia. My professional journey has brought me full circle, now working as a faculty member in the teacher education program in which I trained to be a social studies teacher at the turn of the twenty-first century. When I entered the classroom as a high school social studies teacher in early 2003, the US government was adopting the most nakedly aggressive foreign policy since the Vietnam War. Finding my way as an early career social studies teacher during this time—teaching content directly related to civics, government, and American history—required thoughtful reflections on my beliefs about the capacities of schools to instill a global perspective in young people.

As I crafted an educational philosophy that rang true to my convictions while running contrary to prevailing nationalistic wartime sentiments, I pondered the origins of *my* global perspective, and whether schools alone were up to the task of preparing global citizens. Why was I so interested in having students examine the geopolitical context of American foreign policy in the late-twentieth century, despite the risks of criticism from parents and administrators? Why was I helping my students challenge the Orientalist binaries that pervaded media coverage of two wars in the Middle East, when doing so could be labeled "enabling terrorism"? I did not think of myself as a rebel teacher or a fearless truth-teller; these were considerations that came instinctively to me when thinking about goals for my students. I came to recognize powerful out-of-school experiences as instructive in developing my global perspective, and as a scholar, I have aimed to examine similar experiences. For instance, my dissertation project focused on the learning that might be possible when teachers travel abroad to develop historical and cultural content knowledge. I have also queried historic museums and archives as spaces for teacher development. This book, then, with its focus on public pedagogy around global issues, is a natural outgrowth from those inquiries.

I (Bill) began my secondary school teaching career in 1990, when I was hired fresh out of my bachelor's degree to teach a comparative world studies course in New Jersey. The course was fairly edgy for its time, engaging juniors in studies of Indigenous peoples, geopolitics, human rights, environmental challenges, and sustainable development. It was a highly atypical course for high school students over 30 years ago such that when I told colleagues what I was doing, their response was one of incredulity. But teaching that course to those 16- to 17-year-olds for over a decade taught me about the capacity of all kinds of people—the course was required, so every student graduating from that high school had to pass it—to engage in these complex issues thoughtfully if engaged in pedagogically sound ways. There were lots of learning activities, from films to novels to simulations to field trips to independent inquiries, that allowed the course to unfold. And that work led me to do field study and lead faculty and student trips to Kenya and Russia over the course of that decade while writing more specialized courses in diversity, cultural studies, and geopolitical hotspots.

I did not realize at the time how much my life's course was being set through this experience as I would go on to earn a doctorate in education with a focus on global education, which I later came to understand as GCE. And while my life changed substantially by joining a university, I kept my reverence for what is possible in a classroom and how important it is to have educators who can skillfully engage young people in the aspirational and future-pointing work of global learning. This sharpened my commitment to working with teachers and those learning to be teachers about how to do this work and thus formed the foundation of my work as a teacher educator for GCE. While I recognize that GCE is a somewhat alien-sounding phrase, I have spent the most recent part of my career looking at how everyday practices resonate on a global scale and how we can educate about the fundamental inter-being of our lives and the biosphere through these quotidian moments. That may strike the reader as odd—how do you move from everyday learning toward iconic global events? Upon reflection, the shift is appropriate and even intentional. The mundane or everyday routines are only because they are set apart from the peak moments or heightened experiences that the global events we studied represent.

Enough about us. Now for the contents of what lies ahead. In Chapter 2, *A Brief History of the Global Event*, we offer a retrospective dating back to the Concert for Bangladesh in New York City in 1971, chronicling similar efforts through the present day. Along with concerts, we consider global issues film festivals like the United Nations Association Film Festival in Palo Alto. These smaller venues raise some of the same issues about which foci are given, and thereby which are marginalized, peripheral events that spring up in relation to the main global event. This chapter gives readers a clear sense of the type of activity that we focus on herein while underscoring the value of studying these mass educational experiences framed as entertainment. We close this chapter by looking at how global events are morphing as a result of social media and their subsequent social networks. How do online movements raise awareness and generate activity on social issues, facilitated by the ubiquitous presence of social media?

In Chapter 3, *Global Concerts: More Music, Less Message*, we sharpen our focus on the global issues concert. Data from this chapter were drawn from two recent concerts to promote awareness and engagement around the Sustainable Development Goals 2015–2030 (SDG 15–30), namely the Global Citizen Festival 2019 and Global Citizen Live 2021. We consider the venues, musicians, and theme content of these concerts and witness participants describing their experiences attending the concerts, which focus intently on building support for the global problems identified in the SDGs and urging subsequent actions of policymakers. But the particular and political message of these events urging people to do something is equal to the universalist impulse championed by the same event, or the commitment to a cosmopolitan response to the problems that we face as a planet.

In Chapter 4, *Viewing, Not Doing: Film Festivals on Global Problems*, we look at two recent film festivals, the United Nations Association Film Festival in Palo Alto, 2019, and the Marda Loop Justice Film Festival in Calgary, 2019. Both of these festivals are framed by human rights discourse and examples of global injustices—from the trafficking of sex workers to the abuse of children in India and Canada, from the ecological degradation of oceans due to plastics to the plight of Indigenous peoples, to name a few. The film festivals are somewhat niche events in comparison to concerts as there are far fewer attendees and those who do attend are very likely to already be engaged in various discourses and forms of activism that orient them toward being global citizens. And despite their global orientation, in both cases, we see ample connections to what was happening locally and regionally that made the events more resonant than they would otherwise be.

In Chapter 5, *At-Home Events: Global Engagement in the Twenty-First Century?*, we shift our focus to the most recent forms of global events, those carried out through social networks and on social media. Here we consider the rise of activism and engagement through social media, particularly in what transpired after the COVID-19 pandemic of early 2020. We highlight two substitute concerts: "One World: Together at Home" that was held on April 18, 2020, at the beginning peak of the new infectious disease outbreak and in what was already a lengthy shutdown of most parts of society and "Global Goal: Unite for Our Future," held on June 27, 2020, as hopes for the development of a COVID-19 vaccine began to peak. Musicians recording at home and celebrities appearing in their kitchens added to the domestic and low-key feel of these events, and yet the reach of these made-for-television events hit a peak of 250 million viewers. We close this chapter by looking at how the pandemic may have permanently reshaped the ways that global events are enacted, who attends them, and the ways that they are mediated through social networks.

Finally, we close this book with Chapter 6, *Learnings from Global Events* wherein we encapsulate the insights generated in these studies and point toward what potential events like these and others yet to be planned have in creating a more robust and engaging platform for public pedagogy about pressing global issues.

References

Bosio, E., & Schattle, H. (2021). Ethical global citizenship education: From neoliberalism to a values-based pedagogy. *Prospects*, 1–11. doi:10.1007/s11125-021-09571-9

Castoriadis, C. (1997). *World in fragments: Writings on politics, society, psychoanalysis, and the imagination* (D. A. Curtis, Trans.). Stanford University Press.

Dewey, J. (1938). *Experience and education*. Macmillan Company.

Fraser, N. (2009). *Scales of justice: Reimagining political space in a globalizing world*. Columbia University Press.

Friedman, T. L. (2006). *The world is flat: A brief history of the twenty-first century*. Farrar, Straus and Giroux.

Gitelman, L. (2014). *Paper knowledge: Toward a media history of documents*. Duke University Press.

King, M. L., Jr. (1967, December 24). *Christmas sermon*. [Speech audio recording]. On Being. https://onbeing.org/blog/martin-luther-kings-last-christmas-sermon/

Mannion, G., Biesta, G., Priestley, M., & Ross, H. (2011). The global dimension in education and education for global citizenship: Genealogy and critique. *Globalisation, Societies and Education, 9*(3–4), 443–456. doi:10.1080/14767724.2011.605327

Mathieu, D. (2015). The continued relevance of reception analysis in the age of social media. *Trípodos, 36*, 13–34.

Müller, K. F. (2021). Beyond classic mass media and stand-alone technologies: Using media online in the domestic sphere. *European Journal of Communication, 36*(1), 69–84.

Pashby, K., da Costa, M., Stein, S., & Andreotti, V. (2020). A meta-review of typologies of global citizenship education. *Comparative Education, 56*(2), 144–164. doi:10.1080/03050068.2020.1723352

Pew Charitable Trusts. (2022). https://www.pewtrusts.org/en/topics/media-and-news

Roemhild, R., & Gaudelli, W. (2021). Climate change as quality education: Global citizenship education as a pathway to meaningful citizenship. In R. Iyengar & C. T. Kwauk (Eds.), *Curriculum and learning for climate action* (pp. 104–119). Leiden and Boston: Brill Publishers.

Rooney, K. (2008). *Reading with Oprah: The book club that changed America*. University of Arkansas Press.

Sachs, J. (2015). *The age of sustainable development*. Columbia University Press.

Schattle, H. (2008). *The practices of global citizenship*. Rowman & Littlefield.

Schrøder, K. C. (2000). Making sense of audience discourses: Towards a multidimensional model of mass media reception. *European Journal of Cultural Studies, 3*(2), 233–258.

Slaughter, A. M. (2004). *A new world order*. Princeton University Press.

Soja, E., & Thirdspace, W. (1996). *Journeys to Los Angeles and other real-and-imagined places*. Blackwell.

Staiger, J. (2005). *Media reception studies*. NYU Press.

Stiglitz, J. E. (2017). *Globalization and its discontents revisited*. WW Norton.

Todd, S. (2014). Pedagogy as transformative event: Becoming singularly present in context. *Counterpoints, 462*, 154–168.

United Nations Educational, Scientific and Cultural Organization (UNESCO). (2014). *Global citizenship education: Preparing learners for the challenges of the 21st century*. https://unesdoc.unesco.org/ark:/48223/pf0000227729

Wang, S. (2018). Music, social media and public pedagogy: Indie music in the post-Cantopop epoch. *Asian Education and Development Studies, 7*(1), 42–52.

Weber, E. (1976). *Peasants into Frenchmen: The modernization of rural France, 1870–1914*. Stanford University Press.

Well-Read Black Girl. (n.d.). *Our story*. https://www.wellreadblackgirl.com/our-story

Wenar, L. (2016). *Blood oil: Tyrants, violence, and the rules that run the world*. Oxford University Press.

2

A BRIEF HISTORY OF THE GLOBAL EVENT

This chapter serves as a brief retrospective examining various examples and rationales at work within global events, demonstrating how the contemporary iterations are illustrative of a wider social conversation about the issues. The lineage of the global event begins with the Concert for Bangladesh (1971), followed by Live Aid (1985), Make Poverty History/One World Campaign (2004), Live 8 (2005), Live Earth (2008), and the serial concert series related to the Sustainable Development Goals 2015–2030 (SDG 15–30), Global Citizenship (2012–present). These various global events were designed to garner attention for particular issues, such as Live Aid's focus on famine in East Africa, while supporting a notion that people regardless of borders or state affiliation can care for and support those other than themselves. With regard to film festivals, the ethos of issue-focused care beyond oneself is similar, but the venue is typically focused less on spectacle and more on learning through documentary. Some illustrations of these—which are far too numerous to represent here—include the Environmental Film Festival (Washington DC/annually), United Nations Association Film Festival (Palo Alto/annually), Marda Loop Justice Film Festival (Calgary), and Global Peace Film Festival (Orlando). Finally, the connectivity of social networks has made the internet a space for concerned citizens to interact, spread awareness, and take action around a number of global issues. Trending hashtags, sharing of news stories, donating to organizations, and engaging in discussion all denote a Web 2.0 form of global citizenship.

Our scan of events focused on those designed to educate and motivate participants to learn about and support actions to address a global issue. We employed criteria for determining which events to include and exclude while recognizing the subjectivity that inheres within this process. We focus on events that (1) are organized with explicit attention to global issues in framing, aiming to raise

DOI: 10.4324/9780429281570-2

awareness and/or influence policy changes and/or spark citizen action to address an issue; (2) generate high levels of attention, if episodic, within the immediate venue and beyond, through various forms of media; and (3) have an explicitly educational purpose that augments the spectacle of high-profile performers or visual texts (e.g., films). We omitted large-scale events that had a primarily domestic focus, such as Woodstock of the 1960s, the Million Man March of the 1990s, or the Women's March of 2017. These events certainly included global dimensions and yet their primary focus was on promoting a political agenda within a particular state or simply being a social outlet for its own sake.

Global Concerts

Chapter 2 begins with a respective analysis of global concerts. Though charity concerts have a long history, we aim to focus on concerts aimed at bringing awareness or relief to issues that span national borders or are distant from the audiences that attend these performances. As such, our narrative begins with the Concert for Bangladesh, explores Live Aid, and then focuses on Live 8 and the concerts that have borrowed from this established format.

The Origins of the Global Concert: Concert for Bangladesh

The use of live musical performances to benefit those in need is not especially new. Composer George Freidrich Handel organized annual performances in support of orphans' charities in London for a decade starting in 1749. In 1918 a concert was held to raise funds for the widows and orphans of soldiers in the Austro-Hungarian military killed during World War I. However, the particular iteration of benefit concert we are interested in, the global concert, emerged in the second half of the twentieth century. The growth of popular music beginning in the 1950s produced the music festival format, which incorporates live performances by multiple artists in one large venue, sometimes with multiple stages and often held outdoors. Throughout the latter half of the twentieth century, the association between music and political and social movements took on greater meaning (Hague et al., 2008; Street, 2003, 2007; West, 2013). In the US, for example, rock and roll and folk music became the soundtrack for the anti-Vietnam War movement in particular and the counterculture movement more generally. Though it was not an expressly political event, the Woodstock concert of 1969 showcased counterculture and protests over the Vietnam War to a wider audience through the music festival format (West, 2013).

In 1971, the Concert for Bangladesh in New York City applied the format deployed by Woodstock to raise awareness about a humanitarian crisis in South Asia, birthing the global concert (Christiansen, 2014; Delwar Hossain & Aucoin, 2017). Two sets of performances were held on August 1, 1971, at Madison Square Garden in New York City, organized by British musician George Harrison and

Indian musician Ravi Shankar. This concert occurred against the backdrop of a fascination by Western audiences with South Asia. American Beat poets Allen Ginsberg and Peter Orlovsky traveled to India between 1962 and 1963, while in 1968 Harrison and The Beatles traveled to India to much publicity with transcendental meditation guru Maharishi Mahesh Yogi. By the end of the 1960s, the culture and religion of India were often referenced in Western popular culture as a means of escaping the consumerism and violence associated with modern life in the US and Western Europe (Christiansen, 2014). As the idealism of the 1960s gave way to disillusionment—well represented by the contrast between Woodstock and the Altamont Free Concert—so too did popular understandings around South Asia shift in the American and European imaginations. While the lore of ancient Indian wisdom continued to be associated with images of South Asia in Western popular culture, in the early 1970s, the region was often presented by these same media through a Cold War lens, where a helpless people could be liberated from chaos or worse, Soviet encroachment.

The two related humanitarian crises in South Asia around which Harrison and Shankar rallied popular musicians fit within this Cold War narrative, but garnered little media attention until the concert. First, the 1970 Bhola cyclone devastated East Pakistan, causing 500,000 fatalities, mass displacement, and food shortages. A year later, the Bangladesh Liberation War plunged the region further into turmoil. This conflict was in large part an outgrowth of the collapse of British colonialism in South Asia. When the British ended colonial rule in British India they divided the colony into two nations: India and Pakistan. The logic of this partition rested on religious lines, with India uniting Hindus in the Indian subcontinent and Pakistan uniting Muslims in the politically enjoined territorial regions of East Pakistan and West Pakistan. This partition of the subcontinent did not account for linguistic or cultural traditions. The people of East Pakistan (now called Bangladesh) predominantly spoke Bengali, while Urdu, the predominant language of the people of West Pakistan, became the state-supported language of all of Pakistan. East Pakistan was further treated as an internal colony, with the Bengali people facing stark economic and political disadvantages (Wolf, 2013). Following partition and through the 1960s, the Bengali Language Movement pushed for the independence of East Pakistan from Pakistan.

The Bangladesh Liberation War began on March 26, 1971, when East Pakistan asserted its independence from Pakistan. The previous year the Awami League, the most populous political party in East Pakistan, won a majority of seats in the National Parliament in the general election. This political victory was due in no small part to the government's ineffective response to the Bhola cyclone. The West Pakistani military placed the nation under martial law before they could establish a new government in Islamabad. In response, agitation for independence in East Pakistan increased, while the Pakistani military launched Operation Searchlight which sought to eradicate supporters of Bengali independence, effectively enacting a genocide against the Bengali people. During the war, the

Pakistani military committed terrible atrocities with more than 3 million people killed and 200,000 raped (Beachler, 2007). Bangladesh received its independence in December of 1971 after the Indian military intervened and ultimately forced Pakistan's surrender. India's involvement sparked Cold War anxieties in American president Richard Nixon and his foreign policy advisers. Despite the well-documented genocide, the US sided with West Pakistan, enacting a form of "gun boat diplomacy" with the hopes of intimidating Indian Prime Minister Indira Gandhi (Wolf, 2013).

Shankar says he made Harrison aware of the humanitarian crisis while completing an autobiographical film titled *Ravi* and asked for Harrison's help in running an event that would generate awareness and monetary donations (Greene, 2006; Shankar, 1999). Shankar imagined that as a celebrity Harrison's involvement in the event would bring much attention to the situation in Bangladesh. He had become world-famous as a member of the massively popular rock and roll group The Beatles. At first blush, Harrison was not an obvious choice to lead an explicitly political effort. While The Beatles' musical style was certainly revolutionary, they first made their fame in the early 1960s writing songs that pushed back on norms associated with teenage courtship and mocked authority figures but were not overtly political (Delwar Hossain & Aucoin, 2017). Some of their later songs, such as "Revolution," did represent a countercultural New Left political alignment. These songs embraced a vision of a more peaceful and equitable world, but one remade without the violent revolution espoused by previous iterations of leftist movements. These political songs were primarily written by John Lennon and though he did become increasingly politically active in the late 1960s and early 1970s, Harrison was not generally associated with this brand of activism.

Because of his involvement in The Beatles' trip to India, his close friendship with Shankar, and his embrace of the International Society for Krishna Consciousness (Hare Krishnas), Harrison came to be seen as something of an ambassador to South Asia. However, Harrison admitted to only having limited knowledge of the events in Bangladesh. For Harrison, organizing the Concert for Bangladesh was very much an act of friendship. In the song "Bangla Desh," which Harrison wrote specifically for the concert, he sings that Shankar "came to me/With sadness in his eyes/He told me that he wanted help/Before his country dies." The event Harrison suggested and ultimately organized would be much more ambitious than the one Shankar envisioned (Shankar, 1999). The concert had two goals: to raise funds for Bengali refugees fleeing violence and to raise awareness about this travesty. Harrison prioritized awareness over fundraising, suggesting during a press conference that awareness was "even more important than the money, because…even if we make 5 million dollars, it's still small compared to the size of the problem, so it's more important to really bring the awareness around to the mass of people" (as cited in Christiansen, 2014, p. 142).

The Concert for Bangladesh would become the first global concert partly because it was the first attempt at such an event at this scale. But it would also go on to be a sensation because of the high-profile performers who would take the stage that day. The Beatles drummer Ringo Starr played with Harrison in a supergroup, marking the first time in four years that any of The Beatles shared a stage.[1] Also performing in that supergroup were Eric Clapton and Bob Dylan, both of whom were returning to live performance after extended hiatuses. Dylan also performed a surprise solo set, including two overtly political songs, "Blowing in the Wind" and "A Hard Rain's a-Gonna Fall." Though audiences were undoubtedly drawn to the Concert for Bangladesh for the performances by Western rock and roll musicians, as master of ceremonies Harrison built in moments for the audience to learn about the culture and current events of Bangladesh. For example, the festivities began with a performance by Shankar and other classical Indian musicians. Perhaps under the assumption that the crowd was not there to see world-renowned musicians such as Shankar and Ali Akbar Khan, Harrison asked the crowd for quiet and attention noting their music would require "a little more serious listening" (as cited in Christiansen, 2014, p. 143). This performance was followed by a film depicting atrocities committed during the Bangladesh Liberation War.

The performances only earned roughly $250,000, but an album and concert film (re-released on DVD in 2005) earned millions of dollars, with $13.5 million being delivered to aid workers in Bangladesh by 1982 (Delwar Hossain & Aucoin, 2017). A subsequent dispute with the Internal Revenue Service over the tax-exempt status of the concert and album sales caused a delay in the distribution of funds. Eight million Bengali children died of starvation in the interim, causing Harrison's disillusionment with the benefit concert format (Delwar Hossain & Aucoin, 2017). However, following the concert Shankar and Harrison both expressed satisfaction with the results. Shankar assessed, "Overnight everybody knew the name of Bangladesh…so it has a tremendous value" (as cited in Christiansen, 2014, p. 146), while Harrison reflected "The main thing was, we spread the word and helped get the war ended" (Greene, 2006, p. 194). The concert itself raised media attention and general awareness toward the atrocities occurring in West Pakistan (Christiansen, 2014; Delwar Hossain & Aucoin, 2017; Mookherjee, 2011), though the extent to which the concert helped bring an end to the war was perhaps overstated by Harrison and other participants. Despite popular support for Bangladesh by the American people, the Nixon administration continued to support the efforts of West Pakistan, and the war carried on for months after the concert. Still, on the anniversary of Bangladesh's independence Harrison was recognized by the popular press for the Concert for Bangladesh, while in 2012 Harrison, Shankar, and Dylan were recognized as "Friends of Bangladesh" by the Bangladeshi government (Delwar Hossain & Aucoin, 2017).

The music press and scholars alike have noted Harrison's well-intentioned efforts in analyzing the meaning of the Concert for Bangladesh and its legacies.

Editors of the *Rolling Stone* magazine harkened back to the idealism of Woodstock, calling this event a "revival of all that was best about the Sixties," even if only for a moment (Editors of *Rolling Stone*, 2002, p. 154) while one music critic celebrated Harrison's efforts for putting "rock music back on course" (Woffinden, 1981, p. 51). One of Harrison's biographers referred to the years surrounding the Concert for Bangladesh as "The George Harrison Moment" (Clayson, 2001). While the concert most certainly brought awareness of and material relief to those suffering during the Bangladesh Liberation War, commentators have questioned whether this format provided a means for Western audiences to understand it.

The Global Concert Refined: Live Aid

The success of the concert, if only from a public relations standpoint, triggered a string of global concerts that adopted aspects of the Concert for Bangladesh. In 1974, folksingers Arlo Guthrie and Phil Ochs performed a concert in support of Chilean refugees and Chilean forces fighting the US-backed Pinochet regime (Sharp, 2008). The concert, entitled "An Evening with Salvador Allende," borrowed Harrison's blueprint: the concert was held at Madison Square Garden and also featured a last-minute appearance by Bob Dylan. In 1976, the first in a series of benefit shows, retrospectively titled The Secret Policeman's Ball, was held to further the work of the human rights organization Amnesty International. Initially featuring comedic performances, these concerts later included musical performances as well. The following year, folk singer Harry Chapin organized the world hunger benefit concert in Detroit with John Denver, James Taylor, and Gordon Lightfoot. For five nights in 1979, Jackson Browne, Graham Nash, Bonnie Raitt, and the Musicians United for Safe Energy collective orchestrated the No Nukes concert series at Madison Square Garden in response to the partial reactor meltdown at Three Mile Island. Also in 1979, pop group the Bee Gees organized A Gift of Song: The Music for UNICEF Concert. The concert, held in the UN's General Assembly and televised live, was organized to celebrate 1979 as the International Year of the Child and to raise funds for UNICEF.

Thus by the early 1980s, a pattern emerged whereby celebrity musicians organized concerts to mobilize humanitarian responses to particular cross-national tragedies. In 1985, Irish musician Bob Geldof would refine the template established by Harrison and Shankar when organizing the Live Aid charity concert (Grant, 2015; Sharp, 2008; Westley, 1991). Geldof became famous as the lead singer of the rock group Boomtown Rats, though he would go on to be much more widely known for his humanitarian work. Geldof was an early participant in the Secret Policeman's Ball, but it was televised reports on the 1983–1985 famine in Ethiopia that would ultimately inspire Geldof's major contribution to the history of global events. Geldof later recounted in his autobiography his jarring reaction to these televised reports: "Of course I could send some money.

But that didn't seem enough. A horror like this could not occur today without our consent…I was stood against the wall. I had to withdraw my consent" (Geldof, 1986, p. 271).

The reports which affected Geldof so greatly were recorded and transmitted almost by chance. Famine and civil strife in East Africa had become so commonplace by the early 1980s, most Westerners ignored the unfolding catastrophe. BBC correspondent Michael Buerk and filmmaker Mohammed Amin ended up at an Ethiopian refugee camp when their planned trip to Mozambique proved impossible (Harrison & Palmer, 1986). Their news reports, which initially reached 470 million television viewers, were unprecedented "not simply because they graphically portrayed the horrors of mass starvation, but because of the public response they received" (Davis, 2010, p. 91). The causes of this crisis were varied. Since 1974, Ethiopia was wracked by civil war, causing mass displacement of those fleeing violence and economic collapse. The situation was compounded by unusually low rainfall in the mid-1980s leading to severe food shortages. Further, the Ethiopian government, the Derg, weaponized the famine by restricting humanitarian aid to areas under insurgent control. While precise estimates of the human toll of the famine are difficult to calculate, it would become one of the worst in recorded history (Gill, 2010; Siegel et al., 1986).

Geldof's initial idea to take action in response to this crisis was in the form of a charity single. Geldof wrote lyrics to a song called "Do They Know It's Christmas?," to which Scottish musician Midge Ure penned music. Geldof recruited some of the most popular British and Irish musicians to record the song, all of whom agreed to waive their fees and profits related to the sales of the song to maximize the amount that could be sent for famine relief. This super group of musicians would be called Band Aid, and consisted of members of such groups as U2, Genesis, Duran Duran, Kool and the Gang, Bananarama, and Culture Club. The song was released on December 3, 1984, and was an instant success: it became the fastest-selling single in UK history (to that point), remained the number one selling single for five weeks, and raised over 10 million British pounds (Davis, 2010). Band Aid spawned several contemporary imitators, most famously the American supergroup United Support of Artists for Africa, which released the song "We Are the World" in March of 1985.

After the success of Band Aid, Geldof flew to sub-Saharan Africa and, after seeing the situation firsthand, returned to England determined to top these initial efforts (Westley, 1991). Geldof envisioned two concerts held on the same day, one in Philadelphia at JFK Stadium and the other in London at Wembley Stadium. However, Geldof's hoped-for audience was not limited to the 70,000 that attended the London show or the 92,000 in Philadelphia, but the millions of television viewers, tuning in around the globe with access to a local phone number to which they could pledge donations (Westley, 1991). Geldof billed the event as the "global jukebox," with some of the most popular American and European artists performing for over 16 hours to one billion television viewers in over 150 countries (Grant, 2015). High-profile performers included Elton John,

Madonna, Run DMC, Neil Young, Tom Petty, the Who, U2, the Beach Boys, David Bowie, Sade, Sting, Duran Duran, and perhaps most memorably, Queen.

In putting on Live Aid, Geldof would refine the global concert model borne out of the Concert for Bangladesh (Delwar Hossain & Aucoin, 2017; Elavsky, 2009; Sharp, 2008). Live Aid would ultimately raise $120 million, making it a noteworthy success in terms of fundraising around a global issue (Brearton, 2001). This sum was considerably more than the $13.5 million raised by the Concert for Bangladesh tickets and album sales. Geldof proved much more adept than Harrison at working the available networks to maximize exposure to as broad an audience as possible to Live Aid. Geldof was a relentless fundraiser, with one *Rolling Stone* writer calling him the "man who wouldn't take no for an answer" (Fricke, 1985). Geldof also benefited from a music industry that had developed into complex networks of artists, managers, technicians, and record companies, more so than the industry in which Harrison put on the Concert for Bangladesh (Westley, 1991). As singer and manager of the Boomtown Rats, Geldof had both intimate knowledge of these networks and the entrepreneurial qualities to activate them in service of his cause.

Of course, a central strategy of both concerts was using the emotional power of musical performance to affect change. Both concerts also attempted to further engage audiences' emotions by juxtaposing these musical performances with projected films depicting the crises to which they were responding. However, Geldof was able to utilize the communicative power of satellite television to reach a broader audience than could be imagined in 1971. And while both Harrison and Geldof appealed to a shared humanity between their audiences and the peoples suffering in South Asia and East Africa, Geldof crafted a shrewd analogy that to "consume music is to feed the hungry," and gave "consumers the sense that where nations and bureaucracies had failed, they could make a difference" (Westley, 1991, pp. 1032–1033).

This notion that consumption might solve Africa's problems reveals an additional way in which Live Aid innovated on the model established by the Concert for Bangladesh. Live Aid was not the overtly political event that was the Concert for Bangladesh (Delwar Hossain & Aucoin, 2017; Grant, 2015). For example, while Geldof regularly harangued British Prime Minister Margaret Thatcher over policy issues on television, the solutions offered during the Live Aid event were not policy-based. On the other hand, the Concert for Bangladesh was designed in part to put pressure on the Nixon administration to relent in supporting the Pakistani government (Delwar Hossain & Aucoin, 2017). Further, using the term "Bangladesh" in the song Harrison wrote for the concert was a political choice to side with the insurgent Bangladeshis in the ongoing military conflict. Meanwhile, the musical performances at Live Aid were not noted for their political orientation, nor did Geldof articulate a position in the ongoing Ethiopian civil war (Grant, 2015). Perhaps no other image from the respective concerts illustrates these contrasting approaches better than the posters used to promote the efforts of Live Aid and the Concert for Bangladesh. The Live Aid concert poster featured a now iconic image of a guitar shaped like the map of Africa, while the audio release of the Concert for Bangladesh presents a contrasting image of an emaciated Bangladeshi child sitting in front of an empty bowl. Though this advertisement reduced Bangladesh to a stereotype "as only a poor and starving nation" (Mookherjee, 2011, p. 401), the focus was on the cause that inspired the concert, rather than the musical performance.

Live Aid was broadly hailed as a success. Aid workers and the media generally praised Geldof's "unorthodox" approach to humanitarian aid (Davis, 2010; Vallely, 1985), and in 1986 he would be knighted and nominated for a Nobel Peace Prize for his efforts with Band Aid and Live Aid. However, Live Aid was not without contemporary and lingering criticisms. Before the event, Geldof was criticized by the medical non-government organization Médecins Sans Frontières for working with the Derg, given the government's role in causing the famine. One exposé found that the infrastructure in Ethiopia was so damaged that food aid could not be delivered to refugee camps (despite Geldof's efforts to provide aid agencies with fleets of second-hand vehicles). At other points, the Derg would not allow aid to be delivered across battle lines in rebel-held territories (Keating, 1986). In addition, BBC music commentator Andy Kershaw noted that despite an event aimed at humanitarian relief in East Africa, there was not one performance by an African musician at Live Aid (Lyons, 2011). Still, the Band Aid Trust would continue to raise funds for relief in Africa, though not with the same pomp and attention as the original incarnation; it would be revived again as Band Aid II in 1989, Band Aid 20 in 2004, and Band Aid 30 in 2014.

The Modern Global Concert: Live 8 and Beyond

On the twentieth anniversary of Live Aid, Geldof once again put his organizational skills to work in organizing a series of concerts in 2005 called Live 8. There were several events and trends that served as inspiration for Live 8. Most visibly, Sudan, much like its neighbor Ethiopia in 1985, was experiencing violence, famine, disease, and displacement resulting from decades of civil war. More broadly, economic development in Africa in the latter half of the twentieth century and at the start of the twenty-first century had declined (Harvey, 2005). In response to this trend, Geldof planned Live 8 to coincide with the 2005 Group of 8 (G8) Summit (hence the event was titled "Live 8" instead of "Live Aid 2"), where representatives from the leading industrialized nations gathered to discuss coordinating macroeconomic policies around such issues as the global monetary system and global food supply. Geldof hoped Live 8 would be an opportunity for "engaging the larger political issues and stakes behind G8 meetings, namely the real economic and humanitarian impact of their policies" (Elavsky, 2009, p. 387). Thus, unlike its predecessor Live Aid, which was explicitly organized for the purposes of raising funds in relief of the famine in East Africa, Live 8 was intended to inspire broad political change by putting pressure on the G8 leaders to enact debt relief policies toward impoverished nations (Elavsky, 2009; Grant, 2015).

Live 8 was planned in roughly one month, with Geldof announcing the event on May 31, 2005, and the event occurring on July 2, 2005. Despite the limited media build-up, Live 8 would prove to be a much more ambitious event than its predecessor. Ten concerts went on nearly simultaneously on July 2 in ten different cities: London, Philadelphia, Berlin, Paris, Rome, Barrie, Chiba, Johannesburg, Moscow, and Cornwall. With the G8 Summit occurring in Auchterarder, Scotland, from July 6–8, on July 6, 2005, an 11th concert was held in Edinburgh, Scotland, the nearest major city to the summit. Over 1,000 musicians partici-pated, with their performances televised on 182 television networks, streamed to internet audiences, and broadcast on over 2,000 radio networks. There were many notable performances, including Paul McCartney and U2's rendition of The Beatles' song "Sgt. Pepper's Lonely Hearts Club Band," a reunited Pink Floyd performing together for the first time in 24 years, and speeches by then Secretary-General of the United Nations Kofi Annan, Microsoft founder Bill Gates, and South African President Nelson Mandela. Several performers spoke about the cause of global poverty. For example, between songs, Alicia Keys told the Philadelphia audience, "I'm very, very, very proud to say I'm part of a gen-eration that stands up, that doesn't just sit down, while the world is being ravaged by hunger and AIDS and the demolition of the human spirit" (Ansaldo, 2005).

FIGURE 2.1   The Stage of the Live 8 Concert in London, 2005, Featuring the Iconic Live Aid Guitar Logo

Source: Shutterstock.

Thirty million audience members and viewers at home added their names to the "Live 8 List," a petition presented to the Chair of the G8 Summit, UK Prime Minister Tony Blair, calling for the G8 leaders to "Make Poverty History" (Grant, 2015). The names of signers were broadcast on projection screens during the performances. In response to these efforts, the G8 Summit pledged to double their nations' aid to so-called developing countries from $25 billion to $50 billion by 2010 and to cancel the debt of 38 African countries (Davis, 2010). Geldof took pride in these results, assessing the legacy of Live 8 thusly: "On aid, 10 out of 10; on debt, eight out of 10 […] Mission accomplished, frankly" (as cited in Burkeman, 2005). Not all were as optimistic about whether Live 8 met its stated goals. Artists who performed during Live 8 saw appreciable increases in sales of their recordings, drawing claims of "motivational hypocrisy" (Elavsky, 2009, p. 388). Damon Albarn of the British rock group Blur and David Gilmour of Pink Floyd argued that performers ought to make their altruist motivations clear by donating profits resulting from their participation to charity. Finally, like with Live Aid, the performers at the Live 8 concerts were once again overwhelmingly American and European, with few hailing from Africa.[2]

Four years after Live 8, Elavsky (2009) offered a stark assessment of its legacy: "Live 8 and its agenda sit largely off the public and media radar barely even remembered as an event of nominal importance" (p. 390). Geldof's motivations were also questioned. Andy Kershaw, whose criticisms of Live Aid were described earlier in this chapter, concluded that Geldof's efforts with Live 8 were as much about "showing off his ability to push around presidents and prime ministers as with pointing out the potential of Africa. Indeed, Geldof appears not to be interested in Africa's strengths, only in an Africa on its knees" (Kershaw, 2005). However, these appraisals may be overly harsh. It is true that the G8's promise of $50 billion in aid fell short by $20 billion. But a decade after Live 8, 36 nations had their debts forgiven (accounting for $116 billion in forgiven debt total according to the International Monetary Fund). African nations that had their debts forgiven saw 40% increases in spending on education and 70% increases in spending on healthcare (Forrest, 2015).

Beyond bringing awareness and material relief, Geldof's efforts have solidified the global concert as a highly visible strategy for responding to global crises and a forum for celebrities and spectators to take part in a type of global citizenship (Rojek, 2013). For example, in the summer of 1988, the Free Nelson Mandela Concert (also referred to as Freedomfest and Mandela Day) was held at Wembley Stadium in London and broadcast to an estimated 600 million people worldwide in honor of the then-imprisoned South African leader's 70th birthday. The concert aimed to fund Artists Against Apartheid, put pressure on the South African government to free Nelson Mandela, and ultimately end apartheid. In execution, the organizers distanced the event from the African National Congress, the political party Mandela led, and promised television broadcasters the event was a positive celebration of Mandela's birthday, rather than a call to action. Regardless, Fox Television Network, who broadcasted the event to American audiences, edited performances and speeches to remove any political content (Garofalo, 1992; Thrane, 1988), and in 1990, American television broadcasters refused to air the second Mandela concert out of concern for the political character of the event (Schechter, 1990). The Mandela concerts infused the approach of Live Aid with explicitly political goals, making it a direct legacy of Geldof's efforts and the broader "charity rock" phenomenon (Garofalo, 1992; Sharp, 2008). Musicians looking to gain financial support and bring awareness to local and national issues, most famously Farm Aid, were also inspired by the charity concert template fashioned by Geldof in putting on Live Aid.

Like Live Aid, Live 8 has had its own more recent imitators. For example, in July of 2007, the Live Earth event was held in an effort to raise awareness of the risks associated with global climate change. The concert borrowed heavily from Geldof's format with multiple venues hosting televised concerts on the same day. Audience members were asked to follow a 7-point pledge aimed at curbing their own carbon footprint and taking political action around climate change. The organizers of Live Earth, which included former US Vice President Al Gore, aimed to be more ambitious than Live 8, holding concerts on all seven continents. Though the name "Live Earth" was an allusion to Live Aid and Live 8, Geldof was not involved in this effort. He expressed frustration with the name choice, and also with what he perceived as the event's lack of concrete goals relating to policy change (NME, 2007). The most recent incarnation of the global concert is the Global Citizenship Festival, which has run annually since 2012. Organized by the Global Poverty Project, the Global Citizenship Festival has aligned itself with the United Nations' SDG 15–30. We explore the Global Citizenship Festival in detail in the following chapter.

Global Film Festivals

In this section of Chapter 2, we explore the evolution of film festivals, beginning with their fashionable and exclusive European origins and leading to the current array of formats, sizes, and locations. The narrative we offer here is by no means exhaustive. Rather, we briefly consider the history of film festivals, offering an explanation of how thematic, global festivals emerged roughly around the 1980s. We then provide characteristics and examples of thematic global film festivals, as well as a summary of critiques of this format made by previous scholars.[3]

Origins and Purposes of Film Festivals

At their core, film festivals are simply venues where filmmakers first present their films to a viewing audience (Wollen, 1997). But they also serve a broader array of purposes in celebrating the art of cinema. They exist primarily to showcase noteworthy fiction and nonfiction projects and generate discourse around cinematic techniques and the business of filmmaking. Films that run at film festivals do not share uniform characteristics, but they "tend to be non-Hollywood, artistic, serious, and edgy" (Wong, 2011, p. 6). Gilles Jacob, French film critic and president of the prestigious Cannes Film Festival from 2001 to 2014, described Cannes as an effort "to take the pulse of world cinema once a year." He elaborated further by explaining his hopes for future film festivals to

> promote a type of cinema that's both artistic and of wide appeal. To show-case striking and difficult works that wouldn't otherwise get the attention they deserve. To give the people behind a film the chance to meet the world's press. To generate miles of free publicity for the films taking part, enough to stretch from Paris to Los Angeles.
>
> *(as cited in Elley, 1997, p. S6)*

Jacob's vision for film festivals is notable due to the influence he commands as an organizer of one of the world's most celebrated film festivals. It is a vision that reflects the essential roots of film festivals as an impulse to celebrate and promote cutting-edge artistic representations in film.

Film festivals emerged as a European phenomenon, the first being held primarily in Monaco on the French Riviera in 1898. The geopolitical situation preceding and following World War II worked in concert with technological advances in filmmaking to establish the characteristics associated with modern film festivals (de Valck, 2007). In the early 1930s, sound-on-film technology precipitated the decline of silent film in favor of sound film (Marks, 1997). The introduction of sound into films created a challenge around language, necessitating the dubbing or subtitling of films to exhibit them to audiences beyond the nation in which they were produced. This issue of language in films was further exacerbated by the rise of nationalist governments throughout Europe in the 1930s. Nationalist regimes in Europe extolled their national histories, cultures, and languages at the expense of other nations and Indigenous minorities. Filmmakers were discouraged from collaborating across national borders and were co-opted by governments in using their talents to produce propaganda films. Cosmopolitan avant-garde films, which were created and supported by intellectual elites, dominated early experiments in the film festival format but were ill-prepared to respond to these changes (de Valck, 2007).

In 1932, the Venice Film Festival would fill this void and establish the archetype which other film festivals would emulate. At Venice, nations were invited to submit their finest films in a contest where language differences were an "unproblematic 'given' in the cultural competition between film-producing nations" (de Valck, 2007, p. 24). Venice was also unique in that it was held annually, framed as a dazzling international celebration of films attended by elites—features that would largely define film festivals throughout the twentieth century. Going further, the Motion Picture Producers and Distributors of America represented the American contributions at Venice. As a result, commercially successful Hollywood films showed next to European avant-garde films. Venice was embracing both the commercialism of Hollywood filmmaking while still aiming for cultural enlightenment through film. The endurance of Venice's model is owed in large part to its ability to balance the seemingly diametrically opposed "model of avant-garde artisanship" and the "market forces within the cultural economy" (de Valck, 2007, p. 25).

By 1936 the Venice Film Festival came to serve as a proxy for the Fascist Party of Italy (e.g., from 1934 through 1942, Venice's top prize was the Mussolini Cup). In response to the 1938 Venice Film Festival, where Italian and German contributions were over-represented in the top prizes, representatives from the French, American, and British film industries established the Cannes Film Festival (Museum of Modern Art, 1992; Wong, 2011). Cannes was meant to be a truly international film festival in the sense that representatives of national film industries were invited to contribute the best cinematic achievements from their nations. Plans to hold a film festival at Cannes were postponed until 1946 after the conclusion of World War II. Though resort towns such as Cannes remained a primary venue for film festivals thereafter, in the 1950s cultural centers such as Edinburgh and Brussels entered the fray as sites for film festivals. The development of the Berlin International Film Festival in 1951, later known as Berlinale, is especially illustrative of the ways in which geopolitical considerations came to push the purposes of film festivals beyond celebrations of cinematic achievements (de Valck, 2007, p. 42).

Globalization and Film Festivals

Berlin, a city devastated by World War II and divided between East and West by the Cold War, could not hope to draw the type of pomp and glamor found in Riviera towns where previous film festivals were established. Rather, the "distinct political and ideological agenda of its early years separated it from its more overtly commercial equivalents in France and Italy" (Fehrenbach, 1995, p. 236). In part, the Berlin International Film Festival, or Berlinale, was founded to re-establish a German film industry tarnished by its collaboration with the Nazi regime. However, the festival also took on geopolitical aspirations inspired by Cold War diplomatic rivalries. One of the festival's organizers, Oscar Martay, who was a film officer of the Information Services Branch of the Office of the US High Commissioner for Germany, lobbied for the festival to be held in June of 1951 so as to coincide with the International Youth Festival being held in East Berlin. At this point, the Berlin Wall had yet to be built and those in East Berlin still had access to West Berlin. Martay argued for this timing on the weight of this "political consideration alone," as the film festival would "present a peaceful demonstration of the cultural offerings of the Western world" (as cited in Fehrenbach, 1995, p. 239). The organizers frequently contrasted Berlin with festivals in Cannes and Venice as a popular, rather than an elite, event and organized autograph sessions and a parade of film stars to attract a mass audience.

Other post-World War II forces would come to irrevocably influence the landscape of film festivals. The forces of globalization, propelled after World War II by the Bretton Woods Conference, the General Agreement on Tariffs and Trade, and the establishment of the United Nations, led to the emergence of non-European film festivals, a parallel to a similar phenomenon occurring in education for global citizenship addressed in Chapter 1 (Wong, 2011). Between 1954 and 1959, Sydney, San Francisco, and Mar del Plata, Argentina, all established renowned film festivals. Simultaneously New York came to replace Western Europe as the center of avant-garde filmmaking (Wollen, 1982). The years following World War II marked an "extraordinary period" for underground filmmaking in the US, wherein American filmmakers sought to challenge the "home-grown industrial and cultural industry" of Hollywood as well as the European avant-garde (Rees, 1999, p. 57). Thus, the emergence of an American avant-garde, the geopolitical aspirations of Berlinale, and the broader effects of globalization together allowed for alternative exhibition sites outside of the elite film festival circuit.

Subsequently, the late 1950s and early 1960s would see a sense of malaise surround the elite film festival circuit. French film critics disparaged the Cannes Film Festival in particular for the attention paid to glitz and glamor as opposed to supporting new and innovative filmmaking (de Valck, 2007). In 1968, against the backdrop of mass demonstrations relating to the Vietnam War and labor issues, this discontent would boil over into full-fledged protests at Cannes, closing the festival completely. The protests at Cannes would have lasting effects, throwing into question the purposes and format of the major film festivals (Stapleton & Robinson, 1983). Cannes and Berlinale founded parallel selections for films "deemed too radical, marginal, or young for official selection" while the director of Venice attempted to position the festival in opposition to the commercialism of Hollywood (de Valck, 2007, p. 63). In general, these festivals unmoored their selection processes from national film industries by allowing production companies and individual directors to submit their films for consideration.

Decolonization in the second half of the twentieth century would also influence the development of film festivals in profound ways. The reforms at Cannes, Berlinale, and Venice led to greater interest in showing films representing national liberation movements in the Global South (Shohat & Stam, 2014). For example, Berlinale's parallel festival, *Das Internationales Forum des Jungen Films* (henceforth referred to as *Forum*), was imbued with a sense of discovery by festival programmers. de Valck (2007) notes that the *Forum* programmers were motivated by a mix of genuine "concern for socio-political power struggles" in the Global South and a paternalistic desire to provide festival-goers with an encounter with an exotic *other* that competing festivals could not (p. 71). Beginning in

1972, the International Film Festival Rotterdam would take the lead in bringing Asian films specifically and films from the Global South more generally to European film festivals with an aim toward educating the public about relevant political issues (de Valck, 2007; Wong, 2011). Similarly, in 1975, the Pesaro Film Festival in Italy was noted for its showing of militant and politically controversial films from Latin America. Pesaro was also significant for its alternative format, eschewing juries and prizes for publications and audience participation. Together these transformations opened the door for thematic film festivals (Burton, 1975; de Valck, 2007), such as those we examine in Chapter 4.

By the 1980s, there was a total dissemination of film festivals around the world, challenging the global hegemony of elite European film festivals. During this time, film festivals became nearly ubiquitous, occurring at all times of the year and throughout the world. The spatial reconfigurations of globalization allowed film festivals to proliferate globally and weakened the "natural claim of exclusivity of some festivals and a definite end to the European monopoly" (de Valck, 2007, p. 70). Still, Shohat and Stam (2014) have noted the ways in which this new arrangement has tended to reify power relations along the familiar North/South axis. Film festivals in large European and American cities continued to command the attention of the most renowned filmmakers, while film festivals in Latin America, Asia, and Africa were generally passed over even by Indigenous filmmakers whose work commanded international clout. Malian filmmaker Manthia Diawara observed the "ghettoization" of African films, singling out the elite film festivals for contributing to a pernicious problem: "African cinema exists in exile, with more African films seen in Europe and America than Africa" (Diawara, 1993, p. 24).

de Valck (2007) identifies two conditions that allowed for the establishment of thematic film festivals as a permanent feature of the cinematic world. The first relates to the need for venues to showcase films inspired by the movement against the Vietnam War and revolutionary national liberation struggles beginning in the 1960s. As previously noted, elite film festivals created parallel selections for critical and underground films, while other European festivals such as Rotterdam and Pesaro established themselves by showcasing films produced in the Global South. The thematic film festival format was further encouraged by the "political emancipation of minority groups" in the US and Europe (de Valck, 2007, p. 178). For example, the San Francisco Gay and Lesbian Festival in 1977 had the financial backing to attract filmmakers and put on a festival, while also borrowing features from Pesaro, such as roundtable discussions of the films and related issues. Thematic film festivals "shunned the traditional competition format, favoring open debates and critical analyses over jury deliberations and prestigious prizes" (de Valck, 2007, p. 179). Secondly, the sheer number of films produced each year necessitated alternative outlets for their dissemination. While this book is concerned primarily with thematic festivals centered on global issues, there are festivals showcasing films unified by any number of genres and topics. This is a film festival format quite different from Jacob's vision for Cannes, where the *raison d'être* is showcasing both artistic merit and political message.

In sum, film festivals began as events celebrating national cinematic achievements. They were primarily European and elite affairs. Following World War II, Cold War geopolitical considerations and globalization inspired film festivals outside of European resort towns. Crucially, during the 1960s and 1970s, mass protests in the Global North and decolonization movements disrupted the established film festival format and invited participation by filmmakers from the Global South in elite film festivals. Meanwhile, film festivals became ubiquitous around the world by the 1980s. Due to the sheer number of films produced each year, many festivals were organized according to theme, many of them concerning themselves with spreading awareness about and action around global issues. In Chapter 4, we examine two recurring film festivals that eschew the passive viewing of spectators for the cultivation of meaningful engagement with the films and the global issues they portray.

Global Events and Twenty-First-Century Engagement

What we seek to better understand in this section are not in-person events in the same sense as concerts and film festivals, as individuals who participate in social networks are not meeting face-to-face to observe a performance or production. In fact, during social network events, the spectators are at times creating the content shared on the internet, thus making them both performers and spectators. We conceptualize global social network events as moments where a critical mass of citizens in a variety of locales are united through social networks around a particular global issue. As we have noted earlier in this chapter, organizers of modern global concerts and film festivals have sought to further the reach of their events through the utilization of social networks. By allowing for connectivity and interaction without face-to-face contact, social networks have effectively expanded the boundaries of what has traditionally been considered an event.

A History of Social Networks

It is important that we delineate between two interrelated but distinct concepts: social networks and social media. Social media refers to the types of electronic communication—websites, mobile applications, etc.—that facilitate the sharing of content through the internet. Social networks allow users to:

> (1) construct a public or semi-public profile within a bounded system, (2) articulate a list of other users with whom they share a connection, and (3) view and traverse their list of connections and those made by others within the system. The nature and nomenclature of these connections may vary from site to site.
>
> *(boyd & Ellison, 2007, p. 211)*

Thus, social media are the motors that power social networks in the creation, maintenance, and display of virtual relationships spanning distances great and small. To avoid confusion, in this chapter and elsewhere we have applied the blanket term "social network" when describing and analyzing attempts to effect change around global issues across a variety of social media sites and applications.

Compared to global concerts and global film festivals, both of which began roughly in the late twentieth century, global social network events have a relatively truncated history. That is not to say attempts to develop social networks are entirely new; the telegraph, telephone, and radio were all endeavors to cultivate exchanges of content over long distances and thereby create nodes in networked communication. As boyd and Ellison (2007) note, what makes social networks distinct is not the attempt to connect with other people over long distances, but rather the ways in which social network sites make the networks visible to participants. Participants create visible profiles that articulate descriptors of themselves (often including a profile picture or avatar) and exhibit a list of connections (e.g., "friends" on Facebook or "followers" on Twitter). Members of social networks also have the ability to interact with the content created and shared by fellow network members in the form of comments. Members might share news articles, videos, photographs, personal opinions, etc., which can then be shared and interacted with by broader audiences in a social network.

The process that would lead to the development of social networks began in the 1960s with the invention of email. However, because the internet would not be widely available until 1991, accessing email services was consequently very expensive and used only by a small number of people (Rimskii, 2010). During the 1970s, through a modem and a telephone line, users began sharing news and opinions on virtual, text-based bulletin boards. The 1980s saw the development of a variety of online communities, such as The WELL, GEnie, and Listserv. All of these advances had the effect of simplifying the process by which people could share information and commentary across the globe through internet applications (Edosomwan et al., 2011). For example, Listserv made it possible for users to send emails to multiple recipients on a list (as opposed to manually managing lists of recipients). It was also during this period that real-time chat functions were developed where users engaged in instantaneous online, text-based conversations.

These applications allowed for greater communication and digital interaction and would serve as precursors to modern social networks. It was not until the late 1990s that global social network events as we currently understand them became possible (Edosomwan et al., 2011; van Dijck, 2013). The production of inexpensive personal computers meant more individuals connected their homes to internet services. The introduction of blogs (formally known as "weblogs"), online diary-styled forums supported by web publishing tools, meant that people without experience in computer programming could create and share content on the internet around a variety of topics. Though blogs would later become a platform for social networks, early blogs did not have features that allowed for interactions between users, an essential feature of social networks. According to boyd and Ellison (2007), the first social network site where users created profiles, displayed lists of connections, and interacted with each other in a virtual space was SixDegrees.com in 1997.

Imitators followed suit, creating social networks for friendship more broadly or niche interests, such as reviewing products, dating, sharing music files, and advocating for public policy (Edosomwan et al., 2011).[4] Such examples were BlackPlanet, MoveOn, AsianAvenue, and MiGente. These first social network sites were part of what is now called Web 2.0, the evolution of the World Wide Web toward greater participation in the internet due to ease of use and the dissemination of user-generated content. This shift marked an "emphasis from providing a utility to providing a customized service—a transformation akin to the change from delivering water through pipelines to distributing bottled Evian water or a water-filtering system" (van Dijck, 2013, p. 6). Another wave of social network sites crested at the turn of the twentieth century with the arrival of LiveJournal (1999), Wikipedia (2001), Myspace (2003), LinkedIn (2003), Facebook (2004), YouTube (2005), and Twitter (2006).

Social Networks: How Do They Connect and Inform?

Social networks drew broad audiences and quickly proliferated wherever there was internet access. Rather than catalog and describe the vast number of social network sites formerly and currently in operation, in this section, we focus on the three platforms that have led the way in hosting global social network events: Facebook, Twitter, and YouTube. Though we treat each social network distinctly, it will become immediately clear that there are no distinct boundaries in the virtual spaces that these platforms occupy. These social network sites are "regarded as experiments in online citizenship and a reinvention of the rules for democratic governance" since these platforms were "alternative spaces, free from corporate and government constraints" (van Dijck, 2013, p. 15). Of course, in practice most social networks are owned by corporate groups; the rhetoric of putting users over profits in many cases is only rhetoric (de Peuter & Dyer-Witheford, 2005; Milberry & Anderson, 2009; Skågeby, 2009). Perhaps a more sinister concern is the possibility that these networks provide sophisticated surveillance for government and corporate entities, quietly gathering information on the lives of unsuspecting users. Though these criticisms of social networks are worthy avenues of inquiry, we will not take them up here. Rather, in this book we are interested in social networks as platforms for global events, often initiated by users (be they individuals or organizations operating through their profiles) using the openness and connectivity of social networks to engage, educate, and organize around global issues (Jarvis, 2011).

Facebook was founded in 2004 by Mark Zuckerberg in his Harvard dorm room. Initially reserved for Harvard students, Zuckerberg first expanded access to Facebook to students of other universities and eventually anyone over the age of 13. After 15 years of existence, Facebook has 2.3 billion monthly users (Gebel, 2019), making it one of the world's most popular social network sites.[5] Zuckerberg declared the goal of Facebook is to make the "world more open and connected" (Fletcher, 2010). van Dijck (2013) argues that Facebook's ethos of openness and connectivity is embodied in the act of sharing personal information and perspectives. Facebook users create a personal profile, build a list of "Friends" made up of other users, designate particular interests, and post photographs, links, and thoughts as "status updates." When users log into Facebook, they first view their Timeline, which displays posts from Friends and organizations and groups who the user has chosen to follow. When scrolling through their News Feed, users can add comments and "likes" to other users' statuses and photographs. These interactions suggest a "new normative order for online socializing and communication" (van Dijck, 2013, p. 65). Given the worldwide presence of Facebook, this ecosystem of online sharing has altered the ways in which citizens interact and share experiences.

Twitter was launched two years after Facebook in 2006 and has amassed 126 million daily users (Shaban, 2019). Twitter is a microblog, where users share brief snippets of content such as a handful of sentences, images, or links to other sources. Accordingly, microblogs live "halfway between traditional blogs and social networking sites, and are characterized by a high degree of self-presentation/self-disclosure and a medium to low degree of social presence/media richness" (Kaplan & Haenlein, 2011, p. 106). When Twitter users share content, called "tweeting," they are limited to 280 characters. For the first 11 years of its existence users were limited to 140 characters; doubling this limit does not appear to have influenced user behavior, as the average tweet runs 33 characters (Perez, 2018). This limit was chosen by Twitter's founders not out of a particular desire for brevity, but due to technical compatibilities with mobile phone applications (van Dijck, 2013).

Twitter co-founder Jack Dorsey envisioned it as a "generic infrastructure for online communication and social interaction" (van Dijck, 2013, p. 68). Like Facebook, Twitter has developed its own set of codes for interaction within its platform. Users create a Twitter handle with the @ sign followed by a name of their choosing. Academics, journalists, and others have chosen to identify their Twitter handles in public communiques, signifying the depth to which the language of Twitter has sunken into the broader lexicon. Users "follow" other users and will be able to view their tweets when logging on to Twitter (much akin to "friending" someone on Facebook). Users may apply hashtags to their tweets (a pound sign followed by user-generated terms), which act as metadata tags linking all tweets with the same hashtag. Hashtags that are being used at a high rate are deemed "trending" and appear in Twitter's sidebar. Users may post tweets of their own, or "retweet" other users' tweets. Twitter is distinguishable from Facebook in the sense that on Twitter "people follow others not for social networking but for information" (Kwak et al., 2010, p. 594). While the founders of Twitter have touted its neutrality, it is clear that politicians, celebrities, and other famous users command an outsized influence, even leading to a new type of mediated personality, the social influencers. Consequently, the extent to which Twitter has been useful as a tool for bringing awareness to local and global issues remains a hotly debated subject (van Dijck, 2013).

The final site of global social network events we examine in this book is YouTube. YouTube, launched in 2005, is distinct from Facebook and Twitter in that it is primarily used as a site for user-generated content (van Dijck, 2013). Though YouTube has some of the same connectivity features as Facebook and Twitter (among them the ability to leave comments and follow other users), it is primarily a video-sharing platform. With 1.8 billion monthly users (Gilbert, 2018), a number that does not account for those who view videos on YouTube without logging in to a profile, YouTube is the world's largest video-sharing site. Due to its popularity, YouTube has supplanted traditional network television by providing a platform for amateur filmmakers and activists to distribute their audiovisual creations. van Dijck (2013) argues that the integration of features of YouTube, Facebook, and Twitter "simultaneously reflect and construct the emergent culture of connectivity" (p. 111). That is to say, through their global reach and the interactivity built into and across each platform, social network sites offer unprecedented possibilities and limits for participation as global citizens.

Conclusions

The emergence of global events during the second half of the twentieth century has coincided with the rise of economic and political globalization. In the first two decades of the twenty-first century, telecommunication technologies and widespread internet access have helped further establish global events as a go-to approach for those interested in responding to global crises. The range of modalities explored in this chapter—from concerts to film festivals to social network happenings—all arose as a result of media advances that allowed communications across wider expanses. The dynamism between media and message, an issue to be explored in greater detail in the conclusions of Chapter 6, is a noteworthy subtext in this overview. There have always been global tragedies such as wars and famine, but a notable difference beginning with the communication revolution of the twentieth century, was the capacity for these events to be known, shared, and commented upon at a wide scale and in real-time. Thus, a global event necessarily triggers a communicative exchange, one that is also global due to the networked nature of the world in 2022. This dynamic is only beginning to be understood and our exploration of the data in this study will contribute to a better understanding of how the media and message, communication, and content, are synthetically emergent in the world now.

The following chapters extend these brief, synoptic histories of concerts, film festivals, and social networks into the present, a present inflected significantly by a global pandemic and rising populist nationalism. Too, some have forecasted the end of the global era as the pandemic and politics have tempered the hyperventilation of the most recent global period. We contend that this is not the case, that globalization is a condition of life on Earth rather than a new social and political arrangement, though we recognize how public discourse has shifted in a relatively short span of time since we began this work in 2017. The cases we offer suggest the global event will continue to shape public deliberations on global inequities. Subsequent chapters will demonstrate innovations in the historic models surveyed in this chapter, while also revealing persistent constraints on pedagogical goals in the public realm.

Notes

1 The Beatles broke up while still widely popular; McCartney declined to participate in the Concert for Bangladesh due to a then-ongoing lawsuit between himself and the former band members while Lennon only agreed to perform with his wife Yoko Ono, a provision Harrison refused.
2 The only concert to feature African performers was the event held in Cornwall, UK. Titled "LIVE 8: Africa Calling," it was a concert only incorporated into the Live 8 event after criticisms surfaced over the lack of African performers in the announced lineups.
3 For more substantive historical analyses of film festivals, see de Valck's (2007) *Film Festivals: From European Geopolitics to Global Cinephilia* and Wong's (2011) *Film Festivals: Culture, People, and Power on the Global Screen.*
4 In this historical review, we are concerned with those social networks that facilitate global events and have given social networks that focus on other interests, such as dating or reviewing products and services, less focus.
5 There is perhaps no better demonstration of the ubiquity of Facebook than the name of the 2010 Hollywood film that dramatized its founding: *The Social Network.*

References

Ansaldo, M. (2005, July 3). McCartney, U2 rock Live 8. *Rolling Stone.* https://www.rollingstone.com/music/music-news/mccartney-u2-rock-live-8-115876/

Beachler, D. (2007). The politics of genocide scholarship: The case of Bangladesh. *Patterns of Prejudice, 41*(5), 467–492. doi:10.1080/00313220701657286

boyd, d. m., & Ellison, N. B. (2007). Social network sites: Definition, history, and scholarship. *Journal of Computer-Mediated Communication, 13*(1), 210–230. doi:10.1111/j.1083-6101.2007.00393.x

Brearton, S. (2001). Band Aid solution: From the September 11 fundraisers to the concert for Bangladesh, a ranking of megastar rock benefits. *Report on Business Magazine, 18*(6), 35.

Burkeman, O. (2005, September 11). Three months ago he declared Live 8 had achieved its aim. But what really happened next? *The Guardian.* https://www.theguardian.com/world/2005/sep/12/hearafrica05.development

Burton, J. (1975). The old and the new: Latin American cinema at the (last?) Pesaro Festival. *Jump Cut: A Review of Contemporary Media, 9,* 33–35.

Christiansen, S. (2014). From "Help!" to "Helping out a friend": Imagining South Asia through the Beatles and the concert for Bangladesh. *Rock Music Studies, 1*(2), 132–147. doi:10.1080/19401159.2014.906828

Clayson, A. (2001). *George Harrison.* Sanctuary.

Davis, H. L. (2010). Feeding the world a line?: Celebrity activism and ethical consumer practices from Live Aid to Product Red. *Nordic Journal of English Studies, 9*(3), 89–118.

Delwar Hossain, M., & Aucoin, J. (2017). George Harrison and the concert for Bangladesh: When rock music forever fused with politics on a world stage. In U. Onyebadi (Ed.), *Music as a platform for political communication* (pp. 149–166). IGI Global.

de Peuter, G., & Dyer-Witheford, N. (2005). A playful multitude? Mobilising and counter-mobilising immaterial game labour. *Fibreculture Journal,* (5). http://five.fibreculturejournal.org/fcj-024-a-playful-multitude-mobilising-and-counter-mobilising-immaterial-game-labour/

de Valck, M. (2007). *Film festivals: From European geopolitics to global cinephilia.* Amsterdam University Press.

Diawara, M. (1993). New York and Ouagadougou: The homes of African cinema. *Sight & Sound, III,* 24–26.

Editors of Rolling Stone. (2002). *Harrison.* Simon & Schuster.

Edosomwan, S., Prakasan, S. K., Kouame, D., Watson, J., & Seymour, T. (2011). The history of social media and its impact on business. *Journal of Applied Management and Entrepreneurship, 16*(3), 79–91.

Elavsky, C. M. (2009). United as ONE: Live 8 and the politics of the global music media spectacle. *Journal of Popular Music Studies, 21*(4), 384–410. doi:10.1111/j.1533-1598.2009.01209.x

Elley, D. (1997, March 24). Director envisions next millennium of fest: Topper Jacob continues to be surprised by cinema funds. *Variety Special Supplement, Cannes at 50, 388,* S6.

Fehrenbach, H. (1995). *Cinema in democratizing Germany: Reconstructing national identity after Hitler.* The University of North Carolina Press.

Fletcher, D. (2010, May 20). How Facebook is redefining privacy. *Time, 175,* 1. http://content.time.com/time/magazine/article/0,9171,1990798,00.html

Forrest, A. (2015, July 13). Did Live 8 work? 10 years on, the debt burden returns. *Forbes.* https://www.forbes.com/sites/adamforrest/2015/07/13/did-live-8-work-10-years-on-the-debt-burden-returns/#57f3f4b237cb

Fricke, D. (1985, August 15). Bob Geldof: The man who wouldn't take no for an answer. *Rolling Stone Magazine,* 19. https://www.rollingstone.com/music/music-news/bob-geldof-the-man-who-wouldnt-take-no-for-an-answer-50155/

Garofalo, R. (1992). Nelson Mandela, the concerts: Mass culture as contested terrain. In R. Garofalo (Ed.), *Rockin' the boat: Mass music and mass movements* (pp. 55–66). South End Press.

Gebel, M. (2019, February 4). In 15 years Facebook has amassed 2.3 billion users — more than followers of Christianity. *Business Insider.* https://www.businessinsider.com/facebook-has-2-billion-plus-users-after-15-years-2019-2

Geldof, B. (1986). *Is that it?* Penguin Books.

Gilbert, B. (2018, May 4). YouTube now has over 1.8 billion users every month, within spitting distance of Facebook's 2 billion. *Business Insider.* https://www.businessinsider.com/youtube-user-statistics-2018-5

Gill, P. (2010). *Famine and foreigners: Ethiopia since live aid.* Oxford University Press.

Grant, J. (2015). Live Aid/8: Perpetuating the superiority myth. *Critical Arts, 29*(3), 310–326. doi:10.1080/02560046.2015.1059547

Greene, J. (2006). *Here comes the sun: The spiritual and musical journey of George Harrison.* Wiley.

Hague, S., Street, J., & Savigny, H. (2008). The voice of the people? Musicians as political actors. *Cultural Politics: An International Journal, 4*(4), 5–23. doi:10.2752/175174308X266370

Harrison, P., & Palmer, R. (1986). *News out of Africa: Biafra to band aid.* Hilary Shipman. http://catalog.hathitrust.org/Record/000397024

Harvey, D. (2005). *A brief history of neoliberalism* (1. publ. ed.). Oxford University Press.

Jarvis, J. (2011). *Public parts: How sharing in the digital age improves the way we work and live.* Simon & Schuster.

Kaplan, A. M., & Haenlein, M. (2011). The early bird catches the news: Nine things you should know about micro-blogging. *Business Horizons, 54*, 105–113. https://www.sciencedirect.com/science/article/pii/S0007681310001254

Keating, R. (1986, July 1). Live aid: The terrible truth. *Spin, 2*, 74.

Kershaw, A. (2005, June 17). The myth of Saint Bob, savior of Africa; He has carved out his reputation by an opportunistic attachment to Africa's suffering. *The Independent.* https://www.independent.co.uk/voices/commentators/andy-kershaw-the-myth-of-saint-bob-saviour-of-africa-226087.html

Kwak, H., Lee, C., Park, H., & Moon, S. (2010). What is Twitter, a social network or a news media? In *[Conference Session]. 19th International Conference on World Wide Web.* doi:10.1145/1772690.1772751. http://www.ambuehler.ethz.ch/CDstore/www2010/www/p591.pdf

Lyons, R. (2011). The strange life and turbulent times of Andy Kershaw. https://www.spiked-online.com/2011/07/29/the-strange-life-and-turbulent-times-of-andy-kershaw/

Marks, M. M. (1997). *Music and the silent film: Contexts and case studies, 1895–1924.* Oxford University Press.

Milberry, K., & Anderson, S. (2009). Open sourcing our way to an online commons: Contesting corporate impermeability in the new media ecology. *Journal of Communication Inquiry, 33*(4), 393–412. doi:10.1177/0196859909340349

Mookherjee, N. (2011). Mobilising images: Encounters of 'forced' migrants and the Bangladesh war of 1971. *Mobilities, 6*(3), 399–414.

Museum of Modern Art. (1992). Published on the occasion of the exhibition. In: *45 years: Cannes Festival International du Film* (pp. 29–55). Museum of Modern Art.

NME. (2007, May 14). Bob Geldof criticises Live Earth concerts. *NME.* https://www.nme.com/news/music/bob-geldof-21-1345429

Perez, S. (2018, October 31). Twitter's doubling of character count from 140 to 280 had little impact on length of tweets. *TechCrunch.* https://techcrunch.com/2018/10/30/twitters-doubling-of-character-count-from-140-to-280-had-little-impact-on-length-of-tweets/

Rees, A. L. (1999). *A history of experimental film and video: From canonical avant-garde to contemporary British practice.* BFI Publishing.

Rimskii, V. (2010). The influence of the internet on active social involvement and the formation and development of identities. *Russian Education & Society, 52*(8), 11–33. doi:10.2753/RES1060-9393520802

Rojek, C. (2013). *Event power: How global events manage and manipulate*. Sage.

Schechter, D. (1990). Why we didn't see Wembley. *Africa Report, 35*(3), 64–66.

Shaban, H. (2019, Feb 7). Twitter reveals its daily active user numbers for first time. *The Washington Post*. https://www.washingtonpost.com/technology/2019/02/07/twitter-reveals-its-daily-active-user-numbers-first-time/?utm_term=.fa3d1c2af6ad

Shankar, R. (1999). *Raga mala: The autobiography of Ravi Shankar*. Welcome Rain Publishers.

Sharp, B. S. (2008). Influencing American foreign policy through popular music: All the world's a stage. In J. J. Foy (Ed.), *Homer Simpson goes to Washington: American politics through popular culture* (pp. 199–215). The University Press of Kentucky.

Shohat, E., & Stam, R. (2014). *Unthinking eurocentrism: Multiculturalism and the media* (2nd ed.). Routledge.

Siegel, S., Gutman, H., Romashko, T., & Connick, L. (1986). *The U.S. response to the African famine, 1984–1986: An analysis of policy formation and program management*. (No. 2). U.S. Agency for International Development.

Skågeby, J. (2009). Exploring qualitative sharing practices of social metadata: Expanding the attention economy. *The Information Society, 25*(1), 60–72. doi:10.1080/01972240802587588

Stapleton, J., & Robinson, D. (1983). All the fun of the festivals. *Films and Filming, 345*, 14–16.

Street, J. (2003). 'Fight the power': The politics of music and the music of politics. *Government and Opposition, 38*(1), 113–130.

Street, J. (2007). Breaking the silence: Music's role in political thought and action. *Critical Review of International Social and Political Philosophy, 10*(3), 321–337. doi:10.1080/13698230701400296

Thrane, P. (1988). Freedomfest. *Africa Report, 33*(4), 62–64.

Vallely, P. (1985, July 24). Bureaucrats, take note; Defence of Live Aid's unorthodox field approach to famine relief. *The Times*, 12.

van Dijck, J. (2013). *The culture of connectivity: A critical history of social media*. Oxford University Press.

West, D. (2013). *Social movements in global politics* (1st ed.). Polity Press.

Westley, F. (1991). Bob Geldof and Live Aid: The affective side of global social innovation. *Human Relations, 44*(10), 1011–1036. doi:10.1177/001872679104401001

Woffinden, B. (1981). *The Beatles apart*. Proteus Books.

Wolf, S. O. (2013, March 29). The international context of Bangladesh Liberation War. *The Independent*, 14.

Wollen, P. (1982). *Readings and writings: Semiotic counter-strategies*. Verso.

Wollen, P. (1997). An alphabet of cinema: 26 responses to a self-interview. *Point of Contact, 5*(1), 5–17.

Wong, C. H. (2011). *Film festivals*. Rutgers University Press.

3

GLOBAL CONCERTS

More Music, Less Message

Global concerts are perhaps the most recognizable of global events, drawing large in-person audiences to witness musical performances by popular artists of the moment. The essential quality of global concerts is the magnitude of the event: the energy and sheer volume of musical performances and the accompanying light show on an elaborate stage all contribute to a euphoric spectacle. Global concerts are not just experienced by attendees of the in-person event, of course. Typically, global concerts are broadcast live on television (as were Live Aid and Live 8) and streamed across the internet. Organizers aim to further amplify the impact of the event by encouraging attendees to share their experiences on social media using specific hashtags. Producers have also raised additional funds toward global causes by selling digital recordings of the performances.

In this chapter we examine the pedagogy of global concerts through two events organized by the international advocacy organization Global Citizen: the Global Citizen Festival in 2019 and Global Citizen Live in 2021. These concerts represent something of an evolution from the single-issue events like Live Aid and the cyclical events that occur annually and embrace a loose ethos of global camaraderie and common humanity but are more focused on sports (like the Olympics) and artistic performance (like the Burning Man Festival) (see Rojek, 2013). The Global Citizen concerts have broad, ongoing goals, putting them in contrast to single-issue events which pop up in response to large-scale crises. However, Global Citizen concerts are distinct from cyclical events, as these represent a specific political agenda aligned with the United Nations Sustainable Goals. These are events with a more prescriptive curriculum, unlike the loosely defined, apolitical ethos of the *Olympic Spirit* or charity-focused values that typically guide cyclical events focused on a global emergency.

DOI: 10.4324/9780429281570-3

What makes Global Citizen concerts a compelling case study, beyond their value as fundraising and knowledge development platforms, is the method by which attendees gain access to the concerts. Attendees use the Global Citizen app to take action toward fulfilling the organization's mission, gathering points toward a lottery system described in this chapter. Thus, the pedagogy of the Global Citizen concerts begins months before the event itself and ambitiously aims to mold attendees into global citizens by affecting their behaviors, using the carrot of a free concert as a motivation to act. This turns the traditional model of global concerts on its head, where the pedagogy of the concert is limited to the musical performances and attendant educational programing, as it moves Global Citizen concerts toward a position of action, advocacy, and agency, rather than spectatorship, far in advance of the event itself.

Global Concerts and Global Citizenship

The choice of musical performance as a means to generate action—particularly action toward a cause that may seem distant and abstract to intended audiences—is obvious and engaging. Music is considered a universal language, a form of "symbolic communication" bridging language, culture, and distance (Burke, 1989; Delwar Hossain & Aucoin, 2017; Miell et al., 2005). Elavsky (2009) argues the "emotional power of a song lyric or melody" has long-served to "motivate individuals, mobilize communities, and stimulate and sustain a diverse array of political activities and social movements" (p. 384). States use national anthems to cultivate a sense of belonging and patriotism while governments also censor music that challenges dominant ideologies, such as the recent sanctions of Pussy Riot by the Russian government (Anderson, 1996). The perceived power of music to foment political and social change was on full display when the Taliban outlawed the playing of music upon ascending to power in 1996, and Afghan citizens played music in celebration of the Taliban's retreat from Kabul in 2001 (Street, 2007). Musical performance has also been a tool in mobilizing for political action: rock, folk, rhythm-and-blues, and gospel artists were inspired by or had their music coopted by activists in the civil rights movement, second-wave feminist movement, and environmental movement (Dreier & Flacks, 2014; Eyerman & Jamison, 1998). Though scholars debate the extent to which musicians' contributions influenced political and social movements during the twentieth century, it is generally agreed that musical performances gave voice to perspectives that were otherwise unrecognized in mainstream media discourse (Street, 2007).

Global concerts have become a mainstay in efforts to raise awareness about global issues since 1970, and these events have enjoyed widespread coverage by the mainstream media. Yet the scholarship about global concerts is nascent, with Geldof's efforts enjoying the most sustained analysis (see Christiaens & Goddeeris, 2015; Davis, 2010; Elavsky, 2009; Gopal, 2006; Grant, 2015; Harrison, 2010;

Lousley, 2014; Rijven & Straw, 1989; Rojek, 2013, 2014; Street et al., 2008; Westley, 1991). Typically, scholars engage with one global concert in isolation from the broader trend of using mass entertainment events to generate awareness and support. This is likely a result of the cyclical nature of global concerts; a cataclysmic event occurs, sustained interest and concerns across national borders are generated, and a global concert is organized in response. Thus, unlike political and social movements (and global film festivals, explored in Chapter 4), very few global concerts are part of a sustained effort. In sum, global concerts have historically been responsive to a particular moment as opposed to giving voice to a movement.

The mainstream media has tended to measure the success of these events in money raised (see Brearton, 2001). Scholars have acknowledged the material relief provided by these events, while applying a more critical lens to the concern over who benefits from global concerts. As discussed in Chapter 2, the artists themselves see boosts in album sales resulting from their philanthropy. Davis (2010) argued concerts like Live Aid and Live 8 benefited the host cities in two of the most affluent nations in the world in both exposure and tourist revenue. Davis (2010) also observed ways in which corporate sponsors like Pepsi and AT&T used their advertising during Live Aid to construct a symbolic relationship between their products and famine relief. In these ways, global concerts "play into the hands of established, semi-invisible social and economic interests" (Rojek, 2014, p. 33) while allowing audience members, artists, organizers, and corporate sponsors to position themselves as "global leaders of a compassionate movement" (Davis, 2010, p. 97). Global concerts are thus a vehicle for entertainers and those working in the entertainment industry to promote particular music and brands/labels by way of a *feel-good* effort to address a social problem.

Global concerts are events where attendees are meant to be entertained as well as educated, such that the involvement of celebrity artists is a key feature of global concerts (Driessens et al., 2012; Meyer, 1995; Thrall et al., 2008; Wheeler, 2011). In the cases of Live Aid, Live 8, and the Mandela Concerts, organizers explicitly sought out mega-stars from Europe and the US (note the global North orientation despite claims of being global) in order to broaden respective audiences. Artists indigenous to Africa, Asia, and South America were left off the bill or relegated to smaller roles (Garofalo, 1992; Street et al., 2008). Some scholars have observed a discourse of "charitainment" where the celebrities at the center of the events overshadow the issue for which attention and funds are being raised (Driessens et al., 2012). In this discourse, spectators are inspired by moving imagery to act on global issues, but their activism is reduced to purchasing tickets, buying collateral products, juicing the local economy of the venue, and having fun (Chouliaraki, 2006; Dayan & Katz, 1992; Tester, 2001). As Tester (2001) argued, Live Aid "turned morality into a leisure time entertainment" (p. 117).

Scholars have critiqued such expressions of humanitarianism as tantamount to a modern civilizing mission, reducing representations of the people these events were presumed to help as one-dimensional, distant, suffering others (Barker, 2013; Christiansen, 2014; Davis, 2010; Elavsky, 2009; Harrison, 2010; Mookherjee, 2011; Reed, 2019). Christiansen (2014) argued the Concert for Bangladesh provided "a platform for youth of the '60s to remember nostalgically the optimism and idealism of the earlier years and reaffirm the moral superiority of the '60s counterculture through paternalistic aid" (p. 134). The film shown during the concert and the promotional materials for the related album and film inadvertently reinforced Western hegemony by defining the Bengali people by their suffering and their need for saving by Western heroes, namely the audience who were attending the concert (Christiansen, 2014; Mookherjee, 2011). Scholars have similarly observed that the lyrics of the Band Aid song "Do They Know It's Christmas?" (Elavsky, 2009, p. 386) and the Make Poverty History campaign, which inspired Live 8 (Davis, 2010), offered simplified images of Africa. As a result, these campaigns fell victim to familiar tropes of "charity, disaster, and salvation which have been the mainstays of Africa campaigns from abolition through to the present day" (Harrison, 2010, p. 408).

Other scholars have noted the problematic nature of marketized philanthropy (Devereux, 1996; Nickel & Eikenberry, 2009; Tester, 2001) and the absolution of structural inequalities of globalization through individualized action (Brown & Minty, 2008; Grønbjerg, 1993; Nickel & Eikenberry, 2009). In critiquing Live Aid, Grant (2015) wrote,

> seeing that Geldof explicitly set upon this task in a manner that ignored any systematic critique of the politics of exploitation, his actions ending up bolstering the very same unjust capitalist system that created the problem in the first place.
>
> *(p. 96)*

In other words, these events serve to maintain the very system that creates the need for global events through monetized solutions to issues that require a fundamental rethinking of globalization. Not all scholarship has been universally critical of global concerts, however. Scholars have recognized in global concerts an enactment of a global community founded on a utopian ethos of care and sentimentality while acknowledging the manner in which global concerts reaffirm the privileges of the spectators and disassociate global crises from their historical contexts (Gopal, 2006; Lousley, 2014).

Methods

The scope of this study is two global concerts: the Global Citizen Festival in 2019 and Global Citizen Live in 2021. We attended the concerts in New York City and watched the televised broadcasts of both events (available on YouTube after the concert). Before each concert, we carefully read the Global Citizen website and related Twitter posts, as well as the tweets of artists performing at the events, to get a sense of the events' goals and the social milieu for the concert. We jointly attended a side-event prior to the 2019 concert that showcased inventions and innovations—called Marketplace for the Future—that was a pop-up venue in a lower New York City warehouse that featured a range of ecologically sensitive products, interviewing a host of staff members present.

At the events, and while viewing them afterward, we took notes of pertinent observations *in situ* while writing internal memos outlining key data points and working theories about the concerts. To understand the motivations and experiences of concert-goers, we interviewed 11 attendees at the 2019 event and followed up for clarifications on certain responses.[1] Prior to interviewing people on-site, we provided them with our IRB human subjects participation forms and explained the study we were doing. We also examined social media posts of attendees who publicly tagged themselves at the New York concert in 2021. As we note, the experiences of 11 attendees at a concert that draws roughly 60,000+ and a much larger online, digital audience would provide us with a limited perspective on the event itself.

Context

Global Citizen, also known as the Global Poverty Project, has been hosting concerts on the Great Lawn in Central Park, New York City, annually since 2012.[2] The concerts were the brainchild of documentarian Ryan Gall, who was inspired by his participation in Austin City Limits. He observed that the stages at Austin City Limits were "very heavily branded with sponsors, so you might have the Dell Stage or Pepsi Stage. Then it hit me that there should be a Charity: Water Stage or the Hope Campaign Stage. I wanted to combine those two worlds" (as cited in Peters, 2014, para. 2). Gall brought this idea to Global Citizen CEO Hugh Evans, who had experience organizing charity campaigns in his home nation of Australia. The pair worked with Anschutz Entertainment Group, one of the largest American hosts of entertainment and sporting events, to put on the first Global Citizen Festival in late September of 2012.

While the initial concert in 2012 was indeed a massive event, with all-star musical acts such as the Foo Fighters, Neil Young and Crazy Horse, and John Legend performing before 60,000 in-person attendees, the concerts have grown in scale over the years. During subsequent iterations of Global Citizen, the clout of celebrity presenters and political leaders who have appeared at the event has increased. In 2015, the concert was televised live for American audiences on MSNBC, and edited versions were broadcast in the US, UK, and Australia. Chris Martin, singer of the British band Coldplay, was named curator of the festival, giving the event increased visibility to popular audiences. In 2016, Global Citizen expanded to other cities, with the flagship concert being held in

September in New York City and a second concert in November in Mumbai, headlined by Coldplay and Jay Z.

Broadly, the concerts aim to serve as a platform for inspiring activism around global issues. Global Citizen aligns its ambitions broadly with the United Nations Development Programme (UNDP) Sustainable Development Goals 2015–2030 (SDG 15–30), with SDG 1, ending extreme poverty by 2030, being a particularly resonant theme across festivals. Different facets of the SDG 15–30 are more prominent than others in different iterations of the festival, though sustainable living, gender equality, education, and global health are repeated causes promoted at concerts, shying away from some of the policy wonk type of Goals, such as SDG 9, Industry, Innovation, and Infrastructure. While Gall has said the festival itself gives "a little music to entertain, as well as education" (as cited in Peters, 2014, para. 6), the broader aim of this project is to inspire action as an entry requirement, beyond informing audience members and compelling monetary donations. Global Citizen explains they believe "in the power of advocacy. We don't ask people for money—instead we ask people to use their voice" (Carothers, 2019, para. 2).

This objective determines access to the concert itself: attendees received their tickets by completing actions on the Global Citizen Festival mobile app (see Figure 3.1). Each action completed through the app earns points for hopeful attendees. Once they have accumulated enough points, users of the app are entered into a drawing, where they may win a free pair of tickets. Some actions from the 2021 version of the app include:

- Going vegetarian or vegan for a week (to help combat climate change)
- Calling Congresspeople to lobby against deforestation
- Tweeting with the hashtag #StopTheBlock to pressure pharmaceutical companies to share the intellectual property related to their vaccines

Similarly, on the Global Citizen website visitors can sign petitions, take quizzes (presumably to increase their knowledge about global issues), send messages to world leaders, and are provided with templates for tweets. Global Citizen boasts "Join the movement, change the world" and notes that, as of the fall of 2021, 29.9 million actions have been taken and 1.09 billion lives have been impacted by people utilizing the Global Citizen website and app (Global Citizen, n.d.-a).

2019 and 2021

The 2019 concert, called the Global Citizen Festival, was branded "Power the Movement," a tagline which would appear on Global Citizen's at-home concerts in 2020 (see Chapter 5). This concert was held on the Great Lawn on September 28 and was headlined by Adam Lambert performing with the surviving members

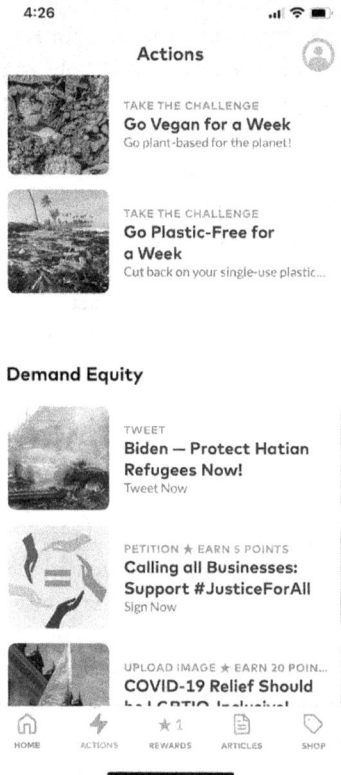

FIGURE 3.1   Action for Entry Screenshot, 2021

Authors' image.

of the legendary rock group Queen. Of note is that this headliner coincided with the release of the film *Bohemian Rhapsody* (2018) and a mini-revival of interest in the British rock group. Queen's presence also amplified the connection to previous global concerts given their high-profile presence in the Live Aid concert in London in 1986 and how those scenes were featured prominently in the 2018 feature film.

Supporting acts included an intergenerational lineup of popular R&B, hip-hop, soul, and rock artists such as Pharrell Williams, Alicia Keys, OneRepublic, and Carole King. The 2021 concert, dubbed Global Citizen Live, was the most ambitious of Global Citizen's efforts, and perhaps the most ambitious global concert to date. Held on September 25 and in the wake of the COVID-19 lockdown, this concert was a 24-hour spectacle with artists performing in Lagos, London, Los Angeles, Mumbai, New York City, Paris, Rio de Janeiro, Seoul, and Sydney. Given its scale, Global Citizen described this concert as a "truly global experience" (McCarthy, 2021a, August 10, para. 8). Artists of local renown such as Nigerian Afrobeat musician Femi Kuti performed in Lagos and Brazilian DJ Alok in Rio de Janeiro, and more internationally known artists such as Ed Sheeran and Elton John appeared in Paris and Stevie Wonder appeared in Los Angeles. The entirety of the concert was broadcast live via the internet on Apple Music, Hulu, and other streaming services. The 2021 concert also implicitly responded to an ongoing critique of the concert series, as it was intended to be global but always held in Northern cities such as New York.

In this chapter, we have narrowed our lens of analysis to the 2021 festivities in New York City. With Chris Martin acting as curator of the event and his band Coldplay headlining this concert, the New York performances were clearly the centerpiece of the 24-hour event. In addition, Global Citizen referred to the performances on the Great Lawn as a "return to our roots" (McCarthy, 2021b, August 26, para. 2). This portion of the concert was also broadcast live on ABC for US audiences, signifying its importance within the line-up of concerts. Along with Coldplay, other artists included singers Billie Eilish and Jennifer Lopez, rapper Meek Mill, and classical pianist Lang Lang. The aesthetics of these concerts were carefully crafted to center the work of Global Citizen, even if the musical performances garnered the most attention. A uniform stage design appeared across all locations, with artists performing under a massive red circle that serves as the symbol for the Global Citizen organization. Inside the circle, a screen was visible to the crowd, as well as a screen that rested on the front edge of the circle. Those screens enhanced the musical performances with glitzy lights and colors and between performances flashed slogans ("Defend the Planet," "Defeat Poverty," etc.). When leaders, activists, and celebrities spoke to the crowd on side stages, their names were displayed on screens behind them. Artists who performed near the start of the event played four or five songs. More high-profile acts like Coldplay and Jennifer Lopez played more lengthy sets of seven to ten songs.

The Crowd

Describing a crowd of 60,000 people is difficult, but here we make an attempt supported only by our in-person observations and our subsequent viewings of the televised event. We were unsurprised to observe a largely young crowd at both the 2019 and 2021 festivals, given that tickets were given to those using a mobile app and the age-cohort appeal of the performers. While there were some older attendees (e.g., over 40), most of the crowd appeared to be 35 and younger. This was a racially and linguistically diverse crowd, as one would expect at a large concert in New York City. Many attendees wore eccentric, stylish, and bright-colored clothing. We observed a number of attendees wearing Global Citizen branded shirts, while others wore clothing that promoted related causes. Most attendees entered the event in couples or in small groups of four. As attendees entered NYC's Central Park Great Lawn in 2021, they showed proof of vaccination and were masked in compliance with COVID-19 mitigation efforts, though as the show progressed many masks were removed. Conversations among attendees tended to focus on the artists: who they were excited to see, when they had seen them perform before, what songs they hoped to hear, etc. We also heard talk about this year's event in contrast to other years. Like global film festivals (see Chapter 4), there may be a core group of people who attend every year. Otherwise, attendees appeared to talk about personal and work gossip; we did not overhear much in the way of conversation about the causes the concert was meant to support. However, by all appearances, the crowd that attended both the 2019 and 2021 events were largely sympathetic to global citizenship causes, though the extent of their activism remains in question.

Our suspicion regarding the superficial engagement with issues among concert-goers was largely supported by the data collected. We asked attendees to explain to us what "global citizenship" means to them given the name and focus of the concert. While two attendees rejected the concept altogether, an interesting observation on its own, the rest offered definitions that suggested that they see themselves as global citizens. One attendee told us being a global citizen means being "aware that different races and religions can come together. Also having an idea that everything we do can affect others." Being knowledgeable about the world was a recurrent theme of participant responses, as was the connection between local and global: "To be aware. To care about things in your immediate and global life." Another attendee similarly remarked, "[I] think about the well-being of people around the world when making voting decisions, financial decisions, resource-use decisions." Some attendees with whom we spoke expressed a self-centered, or American-centric, conceptualization of global citizenship. They articulated concern about global injustices because those injustices might eventually affect them or their families. One stated that a global citizen thinks "about other people in the world, to be thinking about issues that connect to you. I mean if they affect your family and so it is important to think about." Other attendees spoke to causes directly named by Global Citizen: "It means to fight for injustice and to become aware of climate change." In sum, attendees articulated a vision of global citizenship broadly aligned with the stated mission of Global Citizen, even if their explanations were somewhat vague or given to aphorisms with scant substance.

Insights

What Does It Mean to Be a Global Citizen Who Attends a Global Citizen Concert?

In practice, the Global Citizen concerts are celebratory events of global citizenship, wherein world-famous celebrities, advocates, leaders, and ordinary citizens gather for several hours to be entertained and to recognize the results of the previous months' campaign. Much of the educational outreach during the concert itself describes the amount of funds raised by corporate partners and governments and the actions taken by attendees. At the same time, these concerts aim to expand the reach of Global Citizen by putting increased pressure on world leaders. For instance, much of the rhetoric during the 2021 concert was aimed toward leaders attending the G20 Summit in October and the United Nations Climate Change Conference (COP26) in November, and broadening the influence of Global Citizen to those who did not engage with the Global Citizen app.

As noted at the outset of this chapter, the app itself is something of an innovation from previous global concerts. Global Citizen aims to influence peoples' behaviors, making global citizens out of concert-goers. That is, to gain access to an exclusive concert experience, attendees must do some civic work and gain some knowledge of global issues as delineated by Global Citizen. This is a different pedagogical approach from its predecessors, which generally prioritized fundraising and knowledge spread in response to particular international crises (see Chapter 2). It is unclear to what extent attendees' actions are guided by an altruistic desire to impact climate change and global poverty and whether their behaviors continue beyond the concert or whether they are simply motivated to attend a concert. However, that Global Citizen aims to move audience members beyond performative reactions to global issues makes it notable among global concerts.

Even with this innovation, Global Citizen does not appear to see its efforts as entirely novel, symbolically and discursively positioning itself within the lineage of Live Aid. Take, for instance, the 2021 Global Citizen Live concert poster. At the center of the poster is the red circle that Global Citizen uses as its symbol. The circle is split by the neck of a guitar, making it visually double as the letter "C." The neck of the guitar also forms part of capital "G," pointing toward the top of the poster. Thus, the initials for "Global Citizen" form the body of a guitar in much the same way the map of Africa acted as the body of a guitar in Live Aid's and Live 8's logos (see Chapter 2 for a photograph of the Live Aid logo). Both the 2019 and 2021 concerts also saw callbacks to the original Live Aid concert. The headliner of 2019's concert—Adam Lambert and Queen— might have reminded attendees of Queen's legacy-defining performance at Wembley Stadium during Live Aid in 1985. Likewise, in 2021, classical pianist Lang Lang performed a medley of songs that referenced past global concerts, including Queen's "Bohemian Rhapsody" and the benefit song "We Are the World," which raised funds in response to the famine in Africa in 1985. Thus, the Global Citizen concerts aim to take on the mantle of Live Aid and Live 8 while also recognizing criticisms of past concerts that failed to disturb persistent global problems in the long-term.

Global Citizen aims for their concerts to be truly global events. Preceding global concerts have been criticized for their tendencies to be held in already affluent Western cities (Davis, 2010) and to feature megastars from the US and Europe, with artists from Africa, South America, and Asia being relegated to side stages, if represented at all (Garofalo, 1992; Street et al., 2008). While all of the Global Citizen concerts have been held in large, cosmopolitan urban centers, the 2021 concert had artists performing in Lagos, Mumbai, Rio de Janeiro, and Seoul. Each of those concerts featured performances by local artists and is currently showcased on Global Citizen's YouTube page alongside performances by headliners from New York City, Los Angeles, and Paris. In addition, during the New York City concert, which was televised live for American audiences, Chris Martin of Coldplay brought out Zambian singer Esther Chungu to play her song "Jehovah." Martin encouraged the crowd in a somewhat paternalistic manner to listen to Chungu's performance (perhaps knowing a sidestep from Coldplay songs for a song by an unfamiliar artist might lead attendees to tune out), saying, "This is a giant hit where Esther comes from [...] please treat it like a giant hit where we come from too. Okay?" which echoes George Harrison's invocation to the audience in the 1971 Concert for Bangladesh. Due to the ongoing COVID-19 pandemic, some of those performances in non-Western cities were without a live audience, but there remained high-profile efforts to center artists from the Global South.

The concerts themselves operationalized Global Citizen's stated agenda in similar ways, though with different emphases guided by the particular contexts of 2019 and 2021. During the 2019 concert, a great deal of attention was paid to gender-related issues, such as curbing sexual violence, promoting women-owned businesses, education about women's healthcare and family planning, recourse for workplace harassment, etc. Consistent with Global Citizen's mission, the environment, accepting the science of climate change, and being open to making lifestyle adjustments to reduce one's carbon footprint were also frequent themes. The US had announced in the summer of 2017 that it would leave the Paris Agreement by 2020, so this was a central focus of the Global Citizen concert of 2019. This significant geopolitical action was referenced throughout the event by presenters and artists. The sense that the US government was unwilling to act on climate change appeared to suggest a greater need for individuals to act as global citizens, especially poignant for New York City attendees.

Themes that were repeated during the 2021 concert were relatively similar to 2019 and consistent with Global Citizen's stated agenda: women's rights, protecting the environment, ending hunger, and equitable access to education. Actress and Global Citizen Ambassador Rachel Brosnahan opened the 2021 ceremonies in New York by saying:

> Our night here in Central Park is part of a 24-hour global effort to remind the leaders who can make a difference that we need change for our planet and to end the cycle of poverty forever. We are going to recommit

ourselves to each other, the planet, and all of it in service to the next generation. So many of you who are out here tonight, we do not have time to
waste. We need to act, and we need to act now.

A stirring video then played on the screens on either side of the stage compelling attendees to recognize their role as global citizens in ending global poverty,
climate change, and systemic racism. When the narrator, Kenyan youth activist
Eunice Akoth, said "It's time for our generation to realize it's just us," there was
an audible, enthusiastic reaction from the audience. Akoth went on to encourage
the younger generation to protest on social media and in the streets, saying, "Be
the ripple that starts the change."

In 2021, the presenters and artists placed a greater emphasis on racial justice
and vaccine equity following the Black Lives Matter protests in the summer
of 2020 and the emergence of the COVID-19 pandemic. Prince Harry and
Meghan Markle, the Duke and Duchess of Sussex, spoke out against vaccine pat-
ent rules and the hoarding of COVID-19 vaccines by wealthy nations while low-
income nations suffered from short supply. Prince Harry asked the crowd, "Do
you think we should start treating access to the vaccine as a basic human right?"
He went on: "When we start making decisions through that lens, where every
single person deserves equal access to the vaccine, then we can achieve what is
needed together for all of us." Likewise, during her performance, Lizzo acknowledged the historical racism that allowed the current concert to take place when
referencing Seneca Village, a thriving community of formerly enslaved Black
Americans that was razed in 1857 to make space for Central Park. Bringing
the commentary on institutional racism to the present, Bronx-based comedians
Desus and Mero spoke about the ongoing "cycle of poverty that women and
people of color disproportionately suffer from." These themes were present in
the 2019 concert, but the rhetoric around the systemic nature of these issues was
more prominent in 2021.

Global Citizen makes its goals abundantly clear through the app, its advertising, and commentary between performances. Multiple attendees expressed a
nebulous or incomplete understanding of this event's purpose, however. Two
participants understood the Global Citizen concert series to be an attempt to
make them more aware of connections between their local actions and their
global impacts. Amy, a concert attendee, told us "Having leaders from other
countries – leaders that are affected by global aid alongside other leaders – shows
us how there is a connection between what we do here and what lives are like
around the world." Other attendees expressed visions broadly consistent with
Global Citizen's agenda if again lacking in details. Claire said the goal of the concert was "promoting global citizenship: good health around the world; helping
people in crisis." This expression of the event's agenda is accurate, since attending
to global health issues and various crises represents one part of Global Citizen's
agenda, though the "whole package" remained amorphous to some attendees.

Other attendees' descriptions of the event were even hazier, resembling charitable slogans rather than the concrete action steps proposed by Global Citizen. Carson, an attendee, stated that the goal of the concert was to "make people aware of how things are supposed to be," while in Caroline's words, the concert was a "general fundraising effort," without articulating the causes to which those funds would be deployed.

Attendees' experiences abroad or identities as immigrants may have primed them to interpret the educational agenda in a manner consistent with Global Citizen's stated mission. Allison told us that being an immigrant herself, she sees the goal of Global Citizen as "advocating for others who can't advocate for themselves." She went on to tentatively endorse Global Citizen's agenda, because "I am from Africa, I grow cautious about these leaders talking about inequality. Often that leadership sometimes doesn't do anything, so I am optimistic, but cautious until I see action." Allison's comment evidenced a degree of discordance in the messaging behind the Global Citizen concert. Concert-goers attend by right of their participation on an issue, or through direct action. And yet, much of the "between performances" talk from the platform consists of calling on world leaders to act and address global problems. Allison's interpretation very much falls in the latter category—that it is the job of concert-goers to observe skeptically the work of leaders rather than participate directly as citizens—to achieve the SDGs.

Amy was inspired by the goals of Global Citizen, and drew a line between her participation in this event with her experiences abroad: "When you are traveling you can make connections with people who are from different backgrounds and different parts of the world and this festival kind of builds on that." On the other hand, participants who perceived the event to be overtly political expressed a rejection of the event's educational mission. Melissa described the concert as "one-sided and political." When asked to elaborate, she said:

> We are all human beings. I get that, but this whole festival felt one-sided. I wish that they had put America first. I mean we are the cops of the world and we give the most in foreign aid of any other country […] All they did was criticize America, but there is no gratitude for the freedom that we have here or everything we do in the world.

We assume she procured a ticket without using the app, given Melissa's surprise that the Global Citizen Festival was more than just a concert. Furthermore, her maintenance of a parochial, even paternalistic, perspective on global issues despite the efforts of artists and presenters suggests these events might be most effective at preaching to a sympathetic audience, rather than winning over converts or reshaping worldviews. In this reaction lies a cynical way of reading these events broadly—that people come for the concert and are unmoved, even impervious, to the political and educational ends that are sought.

The messaging around global citizenship is, at worst, just blah, blah, blah, and the free concert is the real draw.

The Experience

There is a degree of value-signaling that comes with attending—and letting it be known that you attended—an event like a Global Citizen concert. We do not mean value-signaling in the pejorative sense that it is often invoked, or as a criticism of those so engaged, but rather as an observation of how people come to identify themselves amid the torrent of changes and issues that currently beset our world. To use the app, participate in periodic service over a month, and then attend this spectacle of lyric, melody, and emotion is to say something about who you are or wish to be in the world. That these events are designed to be shared via social media platforms is both for the participants a form of symbolization to the wider-world, but to the recipients of those messages, it activates the millennial trigger of "fear-of-missing-out" that is profoundly motivating, especially to younger generations who are hyper-networked with peers.

As with previous global concerts, the main draw for attendees was the chance to see particular musicians perform live. In 2019, Queen with Adam Lambert and Alicia Keyes were the headliners, and in 2021, it was Billie Eilish and Coldplay. Most interviewees said seeing these megastars perform was the primary reason they attended the event. They also repeatedly mentioned specific performances as the most memorable moments of the event. Some attendees, like Allison, referenced the goals of Global Citizen as a reason for attending, before mentioning the artists: "First, it is a good cause, but also there are great artists and I get to hang with my friends. [...] There are also artists like Queen who I know were active in the fight against HIV." Similarly, Kevin told us that for him "music is the great unifier, people have always come together around that." However, most of the attendees were direct in stating that the music was *the* reason they came to Central Park that day. Amy said, "I guess the coolest part was The Queen concert, which I can't say was particularly connected to global citizenship, but we spent half the time there listening to other people. [...] The highlight was the music." Suffice it to say that without the music, the attendance to hear speeches about global development issues would have been dramatically less than 60,000.

Ruth told us she attended the 2019 concert primarily to see Alicia Keys and observed that "most people are here for the musicians and are just having a good time." Echoing Melissa's complaints about Global Citizen's agenda, Teresa complained about the commentary between performances, saying "I just don't understand why they couldn't have the music without politics." Her comments made us wonder how many other attendees felt the same, but the norms of the moment compelled them to also reference the causes to which Global Citizen contributes. Not surprisingly, the energy was palpably different when the artists took the stage than when presenters offered their commentary. In the case of the latter, attendees typically used this time to talk among themselves. Researchers have documented the power of live musical performance to inspire a feeling of euphoria through an intense communal experience (Baym, 2018; Lamont, 2011; Pehkonen, 2017; Swarbrick et al., 2019). The power of concerts appears to lie in the connection of being with others and the potential for audience members to directly interact with artists (Brown & Knox, 2017; Burland & Pitts, 2014; Leante, 2016; Silverberg et al., 2013).

Our observations would suggest global concerts are no different than those without an explicit political agenda: the crowd is there to see the performances and the activism, and the message is secondary. And not only is it of secondary importance, some attendees would prefer that it not exist at all. Several present-ers made tongue-in-cheek comments acknowledging the attendees' priorities at the festival. In 2021, Kathy Hochul, governor of New York, noted that the crowd came to Global Citizen to "have fun" and joked that her talk would be the shortest speech by a politician they had ever heard. Later in the evening Abdulla Shahid, President of the 76th UN General Assembly and Minister of Foreign Affairs for the Maldives, also assured the crowd that the music would soon continue saying, "Don't worry, I will be very, very brief." The apologetic self-deprecation of political figures at these events is noteworthy as they recog-nize that few came to hear what they have to say—despite the crucial importance of their voices in the realm of policy-making—such that the learning/advocacy/ engagement of global citizenship is a disposable vehicle in light of the true aim: the entertainment of audience-members.

Performers discursively worked to harness this communal energy by instilling a sense that they and the attendees are in a global struggle together, given the apparent awareness of the artists and presenters that the attendees were motivated by the music. The on-stage commentary frequently placed an emphasis on unit-ing the attendees, helping them feel as though through their social justice actions and lifestyle changes, they are becoming members of a global community. Billy Porter, singer and MC for the New York portion of the 2021 concert, began the ceremony by saying:

> You're here, and as you just saw the world is uniting today because you all realize that we've reached a tipping point. And if we are going to do some-thing about it, if we, as global citizens are going to defend the planet and defeat poverty, it requires something radical. For ten years Global Citizen has been in this park, on this stage, with this microphone, and the world watching. We've achieved big things, but there is still so much, *so much*, more to do [...] And frankly I know we can do better.

Similar themes were present when artists connected their performances to the broader mission at the start of their sets and between songs. We made note of several recurring phrases: "artists from all generations and genres," "music unites all people," and "music connects us all." Several artists dedicated their performances to "all the global citizens" and expressed pride at being a part of a global movement. "The movement has always belonged to the people," said singer Lorde before her pre-recorded performance in New York City.

There was a particular focus on empowering youth, perhaps reflecting the average age of the audience. For instance, singer-songwriter Carole King finished her set in 2019 imploring the attendees to take the lead in fighting climate change. Before walking off the stage, King enthusiastically positioned the presumptively young audience as the ones who would need to take the steps to solve the climate crisis, saying, "The next generation and the generation after, we're still here and we're behind you all the way and with you as long as we can make it!" Presenters also made frequent references to the Global Citizen app. In 2019, Adam Lambert noted that attendees "earn their way in. And it's for a cause much greater than commercial pop music or rock music or whatever. R&B music. It's about the world, the planet we live in." We read the repeated emphasis on attendees having "earned" their tickets through global civic actions as serving two purposes: honoring the efforts of attendees who used the app to come to the concert and informing the televised audience about the app. The latter reads as an affirmative form of peer pressure for the televised audience: "Look how many people signed petitions and made phone calls. You can do this, too," while also acknowledging that the message is secondary to the music, a somewhat quixotic narrative about the global concert.

Presenters who are political and corporate leaders and experts in fields served by Global Citizen (e.g., climate science and virology) offered commentary that reflected similar themes to celebrity presenters and artists. However, their between-performance commentary focused heavily on the need to pressure world leaders to act on pressing issues, rather than encouraging concert-goers to do the work themselves. Calls for people to become vegetarian to arrest global warming or to consume less to protect the biosphere or engage in protests such as Fridays for Future were absent from the agenda. The televised broadcast also encouraged watchers to tweet at world leaders to pressure them to act on climate change and extreme poverty, and in 2021, to promote wider access to COVID-19 vaccines. Alok Sharma, the 2021 United Nations Climate Change Conference (COP26) President and Minister of State at the Cabinet Office, spoke about climate change, asking the crowd to call upon the leaders of the G20 group of nations to make commitments to reducing greenhouse gas emissions: "We are all global citizens, and our fates are intertwined. Together, with energy, commitment, and political will, we can make COP26 the moment we change course. We must protect our precious planet." Similarly, Amina Mohammed, Deputy Secretary-General of the United Nations, said, "as global citizens, call, text, tweet the G20 and other leaders. Push them to fund zero hunger, transform our food systems, get vaccines to everyone, and I mean all people, leaving no one behind."

Corporate leaders and philanthropists tended to place an emphasis on the amount of money raised in the lead-up to the event, rather than actions through the app. Yasmine Sherif, the executive director of the UNICEF fund Education Cannot Wait, praised the governments, businesses, and donors who contributed $1.7 billion to their efforts and asked for continued donations. Hans Vestberg, Chairman and CEO of Verizon, spoke on the communication giant's donations to help close the digital divide and to improve K-12 education during the COVID-19 pandemic. Global Citizen Ambassador Rachel Brosnahan praised Verizon's efforts but said that everyone must do their part. They both encouraged the crowd to share their perspectives on the need to improve equity in education through social media. Similarly, the Managing Directors of Sustainability at Delta Air Lines plugged the air carrier's recent and ongoing efforts to reduce carbon emissions. They boasted about Delta's carbon neutral policy and its initiatives around sustainable aviation fuel, which they noted aligned with the UN's sustainability goals. In a short video about Delta's partnership with Global Citizen, they told the audience "we believe you shouldn't have to choose between seeing the world and saving it."

These corporate partners—Verizon, Cisco, Coca-Cola, Delta, etc.—occupied the role of sponsors of the event, providing funds to support the concert and Global Citizen's causes. In turn, each partner had an opportunity to showcase their contributions to the cause and plug their products. The presence of corporate partners, many of whom share a disproportionately larger share of the blame for threats such as global warming, served to foreclose opportunities for attendees to examine the ways corporations in the Global North have benefited from and exacerbated the issues the concert was organized to fight against, or to imagine a more equitable global order absent these global behemoths. The clear message of the Global Citizen concert is that there is no need to fundamentally change the global system or to reconstitute your individual life in light of these challenges—no, not at all. Rather, the message is that you can continue to communicate, travel, and consume just as you do, as long as you call upon world leaders to address these problems, however amorphous those methods of intervention may be.

The crowd generally applauded when leaders, activists, and celebrities took the stage to speak on global issues.[3] However, as the night went on, leaders and experts received more muted ovations, while non-performing celebrities continued to receive cheers from the crowd. Attendees appeared to grow impatient with the between-set talks and more excited for the musical performances. Our impression is attendees at both concerts were mostly sympathetic and receptive to the political goals of the concert as expressed by presenters, but grew more impatient with the educational aspects of the proceedings as the evening progressed toward performances by bigger artists like Alicia Keys and Coldplay. The pedagogical outcomes were unclear if the performance payouts were obvious: more music, less message.

The Results

Though a detailed impact report on the 2021 concert was not available at the time of writing, Global Citizen boasted the following outcomes related to the events on September 25th: $1.1 billion raised to fight climate change, famine, and the COVID-19 pandemic; commitments to plant 157 million trees; and over 60 million COVID-19 vaccines secured (Global Citizen, 2021). These are all worthy achievements toward the stated agenda, without a doubt. The emphasis on the actions taken by attendees to earn admission to the concert, however, reminds us that Global Citizen aims to make an impact beyond fundraising. Attendees and viewers at home were repeatedly reminded that they can take action in small ways to effect change on a global scale. Presenters and artists sought to empower the attendees to act, though what is meant to "act" was not often well defined. During the 2021 concert, Billy Porter evoked Frederick Douglas, saying:

> Eternal vigilance is the price of liberty. My fear right now is that the world is spiraling out of control because we, the global community, have lost that vision. But here today, seeing all of your faces, feeling your spirits, brings me the renewed sense of hope that we can defend the planet, that we can defeat poverty.

Similarly, between songs, singer Billie Eilish spoke about issues associated with Global Citizen. She described how hopeful the crowd makes her, since often she feels like not enough people care about the issues facing the world. She then described legislation before the US Congress related to climate laws and made a plea for President Biden to fulfill the US's promises on climate funding for developing countries. The crowd reacted affirmatively to her pleas for everyone to "do something," the vagueness of her call notwithstanding.

Measuring action and its impact when it is only vaguely described is challenging for obvious reasons, but also makes strategic sense on the part of the concert-planners. Even when specific actions were called for by presenters—most often explained as putting pressure on global leaders through social media activism—how would an organization like Global Citizen evaluate success? Can success be measured by counting tweets, retweets, and likes? Few of the social media posts we reviewed for this chapter took up the specific causes or tagged the specific leaders named by artists and presenters. However, during the telecast of the event, tweets and social media posts that did call on specific leaders flashed across the screen, suggesting some engagement via social media in the manner intended by Global Citizen.

We do not endeavor to make an evaluation of the event itself, though we intend that our interviews and a review of social media posts where users tagged themselves at the event in New York City illuminate attendees' reception to the global concert, similar to media reception studies detailed in Chapter 1. Too, if Global Citizen is too prescriptive in what it advocates, such as limiting pharmaceutical companies' patents on vaccines to permit wide adoption or levying taxes on over-consumption of ecologically perilous digital devices, they would invite even heavier criticism about their goals than they received from this mostly amenable crowd. So the concert-planners "keep it light" knowing that entertainment is the real value they are promoting and the SDG 15–30 are a kind of *leitmotif* that melodically moves the wider event without undoing the fundamentally entertaining aim of the event.

Our interviews and read of social media posts suggest many attendees valued being among people they perceived to hold similar values and ideologies, pointing again to the value-signaling aspect of the concert. Often unsaid but evident in the commentary during the concerts and interviews was the divisive and tense context during which the 2019 and 2021 concerts took place: midway through the Trump presidency and nearly two years into a global pandemic. Reactions to the educational efforts of the 2019 concert reflected a group of global citizens in an American context seeking ways to act in the face of a federal government disinterested in taking leadership on global issues. In 2021, many participants were seeing live music for the first time in almost two years, and their reactions almost exclusively focused on the euphoria of being back together in person following the height of the pandemic. Despite the great emphasis artists and presenters placed on the actions taken by attendees, our interviews did not reflect the sense that attendees felt they were in an exclusive community that earned their way into a concert or that they were committed to being global citizens.

When asked to speak on the most impactful moments from the concert, participants often referenced specific performances first and then described how rewarding it was to be among "like-minded" people. The references to like-mindedness had different implications for different attendees. The reference may have pointed to a sense of belonging and unity, or a sense of hope from the gathering. Claire told us, "It really helps to see a lot of people here, people who have common values. You have a little more faith in humanity." Allison told us she enjoyed participating in an event with "like-minded people," saying, "I learned [that] a lot of activists and the general public are becoming aware of all of these issues. There is so much negativity now, it is like a ray of sunshine to see people learning and advocating." One social media user wrote, "thanks for let me join this movement once again! Together we can move the world doing one action at the time, defending the planet and defeat poverty, so we can make this world a better place..." (FerZelArt, 2021). Another user wrote, "What could possibly be cooler than a festival that brings together artists, leaders, and Global Citizens from all over the world to defend the planet and defeat poverty?" (Pamela, 2021).

When prompted to reflect on the benefits or the drawbacks of large social gatherings, interviewees mentioned the value of geographic and national diversity, as well as the power of large gatherings to galvanize people to act on important issues. Julia made connections between justice-oriented events in which she participated and her anticipated reaction to the 2019 concert: "It's great to connect with people from all different walks of life. I felt that way at the Women's March and will probably feel the same way here." Similarly, Kevin told us he's been following Global Citizen "for a while and it felt like the right time. Now is the right time to be a part of this."

Reflecting on the ethnic and linguistic diversity we observed in the attendees, Carson found it "really valuable to have people from all over the world from different backgrounds, people from all over," and Sarah felt it was "great coming together with all these people from different places." One social media user was inspired by the diversity of artists performing at one event:

> Heart is so full from celebrating live music and activism with @glblctzn ❤
> 🌎 It's a small comfort in the face of all the daunting challenges and inequities miring the world, but being in the midst of 50K Americans dancing to a multilingual collab between a boundary-breaking #kpop group and an iconic British rock band gives me hope for a brighter future. @bts.bighitofficial @coldplay
>
> *(Baik, 2021)*

In 2021, social media users were excited over the prospect of finally attending live concerts again, connecting that euphoria with the mission of Global Citizen: "First festival after this pandemic. A lot of fun, dance and above all let's save the planet!" (Luis, 2021). Another user wrote: "First live concert in nearly 2 years and it's such a meaningful event! We are global citizens and we have only one planet! So, take actions from today!" (Chang, 2021).

Despite these hopeful reactions to the concert, attendees expressed imprecise conceptualizations of how they could act on the issues raised during the concert. Multiple interviewees expressed a nebulous, and in one case a passive, desire to act on what they had learned at the event. Claire told us, "I guess I am interested in doing some volunteer work. If someone organizes something, then I can do it." Kevin, an African-American male, was more active in describing his reaction to the concert, though his planned action steps were limited to donating and in unison with his ongoing activism around racial justice: "I just donate money, that's what I've always done to the NAACP and the ACLU, but they don't do this kind of festival. This isn't the way they fundraise."

Other participants sought overlaps between their activism and professional work. Allison appreciated that the concert spoke to her career in healthcare and advocacy for vulnerable populations:

> I liked seeing politicians and I liked seeing their efforts and dedication. I am in obstetrics and we have a huge immigrant population. I feel like this festival is really what New York stands for: to be a safe haven for anyone.

It is important for health care workers to not judge any of their clients. The first question should be are they healthy, are they safe and not ask any questions about their race, immigration status, if they aren't safe then we do something about it.

Amy, also a healthcare worker, similarly noted that the festival might enhance her work with the immigrant population she serves. She said the presentations on foreign aid and global poverty might "help me understand a little more about where some of the people I work with are coming from and what their families might be experiencing and how that is related to Western and American choices." Caroline, an elementary teacher, told us the concert "might create some inspiration for projects, especially when kids learn to help others near them who might need help."

Other attendees spoke in general ways about awareness of global issues but did not pinpoint a means of taking action. Sarah spoke about taking "responsibility to understanding how the world is changing [...] Things are bad, but people are more aware than ever before." Similarly, Julie said, "I care a lot about the environment and I think this might be an opportunity to activate, to galvanize, just to care about what is going on in the world." Scanning public social media posts that were tagged at the event, we see many selfies with the crowd behind the user or highlights from the user's favorite performances. However, there is some engagement with the global citizen themes attached to the event, even if they reflect a performative demonstration of the user's alignment with or awareness of the goals of the event. One user wrote, "@glblctzn it was all for a great cause and I loved every minute of it. I pledge to do better and be better!" (Rudders Sisters, 2021). But most users appeared to post (publicly, at least) in order to demonstrate to their followers that they were present for the festival or to promote their social media brand.

Conclusions

In the same way that Live Aid was an evolution of the Concert for Bangladesh, the Global Citizen concerts infused this established model with twenty-first-century communications technology and an action-entry requirement, in an attempt to activate, educate, and inspire. But are these concerts limited in their ability to "move from the romance of charity to the logic of political economy" (Rojek, 2013, p. 112) in the same ways that their predecessors were? The artists' performances serve to draw a broad audience to the event, while between-performance programming educates them about global issues. At the same time, the concert is as much a celebration of money raised and commitments made by governments and private sector corporations to solving the issues championed by Global Citizen. The event then pushes the crowd—in-person and at home—to use social media to put pressure on world leaders, the G20 in particular, around these issues. Our sense is that this audience is largely already sympathetic to these causes and may feel compelled to act or are prepared to tune them out and focus on the music.

The Global Citizen app works to counterbalance the performativity evident in prior global concerts, but our interviews with attendees suggest a current of charitainment guides their responses to these concerts (Chouliaraki, 2006; Dayan & Katz, 1992; Tester, 2001). At the concert itself, the app unearthed a persistent tension in global concerts around who can act on the issues highlighted in 2019 and 2021 and what is expected among concert-goers. In this chapter, we observed a discursive doublespeak about global citizenship as embodied in the educational presentations between sets. On the one hand, artists and present-ers praised the in-person audience for their civic efforts that earned them the right to come to the concert. Cognizant of the viewers at home, they used the inclusive language of "us all" working together to be global citizens, inviting those at home to use the Global Citizen app. At the same time, the pleas to act *when framed as outside of the Global Citizen app* most often centered on compelling world leaders via social media to pass legislation and donate funds toward solv-ing global problems. We wondered if these dual messages around how change happens on a global scale—either by attendees using the app or those with their hands on the levers of power—contributed to the charitainment evident in attendees' responses to the event.

Elements of the traditional model for global concerts at work in the Global Citizen concert series are what both make them successful events and limit their potentials. As is essential to all concerts, Global Citizen relies on the spectacle of the event. Global Citizen concerts are first and foremost about the grand show, the magnitude of the performances, and an emotional back-and-forth between artists and attendees (Driessens et al., 2012; Meyer, 1995; Thrall et al., 2008; Wheeler, 2011). Without the spectacle, would there be a large in-person and at-home audience for these events? It seems unlikely. As a result, the spectacle often outweighs the causes championed by Global Citizen, both in how they are presented to audiences and in how they are received by those audiences—more music, less message.

Despite efforts at greater inclusivity of non-Western artists represented at these concerts, Global Citizen relies on megastars from the US and Europe to draw the largest possible audience (Garofalo, 1992; Street et al., 2008). Finally, corporate sponsors are heavily involved in the event, co-opting the message of global citizenship while showcasing their good deeds to a global audience (Rojek, 2014). Despite occasional messages about the structural nature of rac-ism and access to preventative medicine, there was limited engagement with the ways in which economic inequality, environmental degradation, COVID-19, and so on are embedded in the fabric of globalization. Rather, artists and presenters prioritized individualized action through social media activism by attendees, rather than bold systemic changes (Brown & Minty, 2008; Grønbjerg, 1993; Nickel & Eikenberry, 2009).

Still, the Global Citizen series of concerts expands the model of global concerts in notable ways. They represent a cosmopolitan response to ongoing global inequalities, rather than one-off events responding to crises of the moment. This is a decade-long sustained effort, a frequency more closely resembling the efforts of global film festivals highlighted in the next chapter than previous global concerts. This ambitious goal is articulated on their website, where Global Citizen says that attendees will "learn about the systemic causes of extreme poverty, take action on those issues, and earn rewards for their actions—as part of a global community committed to lasting change" (Global Citizen, n.d.-b.). The Global Citizen app works as a pedagogical tool, rewarding global civic behaviors and potentially altering lifestyle choices beyond the event itself. Still, the link between the individual actions compelled by the app and systemic changes described by Global Citizen is thin, if it exists at all. But the limits of its pedagogy one might say are bounded by the broadest of understandings, echoed in the aphorisms of participants feeling called to promote "good health around the world" or "making the world a better place." On the finer points of what changes will be needed to make the world ecologically sustainable and economically just in the twenty-first century and beyond, there is little that has been learned.

Notes

1 All names are pseudonyms.
2 The lone exception is 2020, when the COVID-19 pandemic forced Global Citizen to adopt a virtual format for its concert. We cover those events in detail in Chapter 5.
3 One notable exception was the mayor of New York City Bill de Blasio, who received resounding jeers from the mostly polite crowd.

References

Anderson, B. R. (1996). *Imagined communities*. Verso.
Baik, J. [@jbaik1016]. (2021, September 26). *Heart is so full from celebrating live music and activism with @glblctzn* ❤ 🌍 *It's a small comfort* [Photograph]. Instagram. https://www.instagram.com/p/CUTR_M-gP5I/
Barker, M. J. (2013). Bob Geldof and the aid industry: "Do they know it's imperialism?" *Capitalism Nature Socialism*, 25(1), 96–110. doi:10.1080/10455752.2013.845586
Baym, N. K. (2018). *Playing to the crowd: Musicians, audiences, and the intimate work of connection*. NYU Press.
Brearton, S. (2001). Band Aid solution: From the September 11 fundraisers to the concert for Bangladesh, a ranking of megastar rock benefits. *Report on Business Magazine*, 18(6), 35.
Brown, P. H., & Minty, J. H. (2008). Media coverage and charitable giving after the 2004 tsunami. *Southern Economic Journal*, 75(1), 9–25.

Brown, S. C., & Knox, D. (2017). Why go to pop concerts? The motivations behind live music attendance. *Musicae Scientiae, 21*(3), 233–249. doi:10.1177/1029864916650719

Burke, K. (1989). *On symbols and society*. University of Chicago Press.

Burland, K., & Pitts, S. (Eds.). (2014). *Coughing and clapping: Investigating the audience experience*. Routledge.

Carothers, C. (2019, July 30). *How to get tickets to Global Citizen Festival 2019 in NYC: Tickets are free if you take action*. https://www.globalcitizen.org/en/content/how-to-get-tickets-to-global-citizen-festival/

Chang, C. [@charlesc1025]. (2021, September 26). *First live concert in nearly 2 years and it's such a meaningful event! We are global citizens and we have* [Photograph]. Instagram. https://www.instagram.com/p/CUTuTVVsDdt/

Chouliaraki, L. (2006). *The spectatorship of suffering*. SAGE.

Christiaens, K., & Goddeeris, I. (2015). Beyond Western European idealism: A comparative perspective on the transnational scope of Belgian solidarity movements with Nicaragua, Poland and South Africa in the 1980s. *Journal of Contemporary History, 50*(3), 632–655. doi:10.1177/0022009414556662

Christiansen, S. (2014). From "Help!" to "Helping out a friend": Imagining South Asia through the Beatles and the concert for Bangladesh. *Rock Music Studies, 1*(2), 132–147. doi:10.1080/19401159.2014.906828

Davis, H. L. (2010). Feeding the world a line?: Celebrity activism and ethical consumer practices from live aid to product red. *Nordic Journal of English Studies, 9*(3), 89–118.

Dayan, D., & Katz, E. (1992). *Media events: The live broadcasting of history*. Harvard University Press.

Delwar Hossain, M., & Aucoin, J. (2017). George Harrison and the concert for Bangladesh: When rock music forever fused with politics on a world stage. In U. Onyebadi (Ed.), *Music as a platform for political communication* (pp. 149–166). IGI Global.

Devereux, E. (1996). Good causes, God's poor and telethon television. *Media, Culture & Society, 18*(1), 47–68. doi:10.1177/016344396018001004

Dreier, P., & Flacks, D. (2014). Music and movements. *New Labor Forum, 23*(2), 99–102. doi:10.1177/1095796014524537

Driessens, O., Joye, S., & Biltereyst, D. (2012). The X-factor of charity: A critical analysis of celebrities' involvement in the 2010 Flemish and Dutch Haiti relief shows. *Media, Culture & Society, 34*(6), 709–725. doi:10.1177/0163443712449498

Elavsky, C. M. (2009). United as ONE: Live 8 and the politics of the global music media spectacle. *Journal of Popular Music Studies, 21*(4), 384–410. doi:10.1111/j.1533-1598.2009.01209.x

Eyerman, R., & Jamison, A. (1998). *Music and social movements*. Cambridge University Press.

FerZelArt [@ferzavala14]. (2021, September 20). *thanks for let me join this movement once again! Together we can move the world doing one action at the time* [Photograph]. Instagram. https://www.instagram.com/p/CUdxW8htMcw/

Garofalo, R. (1992). Nelson Mandela, the concerts: Mass culture as contested terrain. In R. Garofalo (Ed.), *Rockin' the boat: Mass music and mass movements* (pp. 55–66). South End Press.

Global Citizen. (2021, November 12). *Global Citizen Live's impact: 1.1B to defeat poverty and defend the planet* [Video]. YouTube. https://www.youtube.com/watch?v=uKbl-kE8Scc

Global Citizen. (n.d.-a). Take action. Retrieved December 8, 2021, from https://www.globalcitizen.org/en/take-action/

Global Citizen. (n.d.-b). Who we are. Retrieved December 8, 2021, from https://www.globalcitizen.org/en/about/who-we-are/

Gopal, P. (2006). The 'moral empire': Africa, globalisation and the politics of conscience. *New Formations*, *59*, 81.

Grant, J. (2015). Live Aid/8: Perpetuating the superiority myth. *Critical Arts*, *29*(3), 310–326. doi:10.1080/02560046.2015.1059547

Grønbjerg, K. A. (1993). *Understanding nonprofit funding: Managing revenues in social services and community development organizations*. Jossey-Bass.

Harrison, G. (2010). The Africanization of poverty: A retrospective on 'make poverty history.' *African Affairs*, *109*(436), 1–18.

Lamont, A. (2011). University students' strong experiences of music: Pleasure, engagement, and meaning. *Musicae Scientiae*, *15*(2), 229–249. doi:10.1177/102986491101500206

Leante, L. (2016). Observing musicians/audience interaction in North Indian classical music performance. In I. Tsioulakis & E. Hytönen-Ng (Eds.), *Musicians and their audiences: Performance, speech, and mediation* (pp. 50–65). Routledge.

Lousley, C. (2014). 'With love from Band Aid': Sentimental exchange, affective economies, and popular globalism. *Emotion, Space and Society*, *10*, 7–17. doi:10.1016/j.emospa.2013.02.009

Luis [@saintluisi]. (2021, September 26). *First festival after this pandemic. A lot of fun, dance and above all let's save the planet!* [Photograph]. Instagram. https://www.instagram.com/p/CUTqWy6sAoe/

McCarthy, J. (2021a, August 10). https://www.globalcitizen.org/en/content/global-citizen-live-nyc-lineup-get-tickets/

McCarthy, J. (2021b, August 26). Global citizen live: Everything you need to know. https://www.globalcitizen.org/en/content/global-citizen-live-everything-to-know/

Meyer, D. S. (1995). The challenge of cultural elites: Celebrities and social movements. *Sociological Inquiry*, *65*(2), 181–206. doi:10.1111/j.1475-682X.1995.tb00412.x

Miell, D., MacDonald, R. A. R., & Hargreaves, D. J. (2005). *Musical communication* (1st ed.). Oxford University Press.

Mookherjee, N. (2011). Mobilising images: Encounters of 'forced' migrants and the Bangladesh war of 1971. *Mobilities*, *6*(3), 399–414.

Nickel, P. M., & Eikenberry, A. M. (2009). A critique of the discourse of marketized philanthropy. *American Behavioral Scientist*, *52*(7), 974–989. doi:10.1177/0002764208327670

Pamela [@psov]. (2021, September 26). *What could possibly be cooler than a festival that brings together artists, leaders, and Global Citizens from all over the world* [Photograph]. Instagram. https://www.instagram.com/p/CUTAU7NJfMG/

Pehkonen, S. (2017). Choreographing the performer–audience interaction. *Journal of Contemporary Ethnography*, *46*(6), 699–722. doi:10.1177/0891241616636663

Peters, M. (2014, September 26). Global Citizen Festival's co-founder explains its birth & mission. *Billboard*. https://www.billboard.com/articles/news/6266492/global-citizen-festivals-2014-co-founder

Reed, T. V. (2019). "We are [not] the world": Famine, apartheid, and the politics of rock music. In T. V. Reed (Ed.), *The art of protest* (pp. 173–196). University of Minnesota Press. doi:10.5749/j.ctvb1hrcf.9

Rijven, S., & Straw, W. (1989). Rock for Ethiopia (1985). In S. Frith (Ed.), *World music, politics and social change: Papers from the international association for the study of popular music* (pp. 198–209). Manchester University Press.

Rojek, C. (2013). *Event power: How global events manage and manipulate*. SAGE.

Rojek, C. (2014). Global event management: A critique. *Leisure Studies*, *33*(1), 32–47.

Rudders Sisters [@izzynabbyr]. (2021, September 27). *@glblctzn it was all for a great cause and I loved every minute of it. I pledge to do better* [Photograph]. Instagram. https://www.instagram.com/p/CUUrL_WLpze/

Silverberg, J. L., Bierbaum, M., Sethna, J. P., & Cohen, I. (2013). Collective motion of humans in mosh and circle pits at heavy metal concerts. *Physical Review Letters*, *110*(22), 1–5. doi: 10.1103/PhysRevLett.110.228701

Street, J. (2007). Breaking the silence: Music's role in political thought and action. *Critical Review of International Social and Political Philosophy*, *10*(3), 321–337. doi:10.1080/13698230701400296

Street, J., Hague, S., & Savigny, H. (2008). Playing to the crowd: The role of music and musicians in political participation. *The British Journal of Politics and International Relations*, *10*(2), 269–285. doi:10.1111/j.1467-856x.2007.00299.x

Swarbrick, D., Bosnyak, D., Livingstone, S. R., Bansal, J., Marsh-Rollo, S., Woolhouse, M. H., & Trainor, L. J. (2019). How live music moves us: Head movement differences in audiences to live versus recorded music. *Frontiers in Psychology*, *9*, 1–11. doi:10.3389/fpsyg.2018.02682

Tester, K. (2001). *Compassion, morality and the media* (1st ed.). Open University Press.

Thrall, A. T., Lollio-Fakhreddine, J., Jon, B., Donnelly, L., Herrin, W., Paquette, Z., Wenglinski, R., & Wyatt, A. (2008). Star power: Celebrity advocacy and the evolution of the public sphere. *Press/Politics*, *13*(4), 362–385.

Westley, F. (1991). Bob Geldof and Live Aid: The affective side of global social innovation. *Human Relations*, *44*(10), 1011–1036. doi:10.1177/001872679104401001

Wheeler, M. (2011). Celebrity diplomacy: United Nations' goodwill ambassadors and messengers of peace. *Celebrity Studies*, *2*(1), 6–18. doi:10.1080/19392397.2011.543267

4

VIEWING, NOT DOING

Film Festivals on Global Problems

Karol Piekarczyk, former WATCH DOCS International Human Rights in Film Festival organizer, writes that the greatest power of human rights film festivals "undoubtedly lies in education, consciousness raising and attitude shaping" (2015, p. 10). The focus on viewing, rather than doing, is justifiable as a point of entry into an issue. Yet, attendance at or organization of a film festival is also a form of doing, as these provide a venue for consciousness-raising about a problem, perhaps one previously unknown to a wide audience. What is the pedagogical value of film festivals whose foci are on global problems? We return to this question at the conclusion of this exploration of two such festivals in markedly different contexts.

The focus of this chapter is global film festivals, of which human rights film festivals are a subset. Piekarczyk's comment speaks to a broadening of the role of nongovernmental organizations from that of engaging in fund-raising and providing aid to educating a wider public about global problems, albeit from a perspective of advocacy. Thus, film festivals are increasingly used as a vehicle to educate around a host of global issues in the absence of sustained formal education on such topics (Muller, 2012). Film festivals are also used as heightened experiences of affiliation that invite those committed to the broad issues signified by the films to enjoy the solidarity of the experience.

Thematic Global Film Festivals

Little scholarly attention has been directed at the relatively recent phenomenon of themed film festivals that aim to educate and inspire action around humanitarian problems, such as those we are concerned with in this book. A number of

DOI: 10.4324/9780429281570-4

these festivals run films in the hopes of bringing awareness to an array of global issues. The Montreal World Film Festival, for example, aims to

> encourage cultural diversity and understanding between nations, to foster the cinema of all continents by stimulating the development of quality cinema, to promote filmmakers and innovative works, to discover and encourage new talents, and to promote meetings between cinema professionals from around the world.
>
> *(Montreal World Film Festival, n.d.)*

The United Nations Association Film Festival (referred to as UNAFF) in Palo Alto, the Marda Loop Justice Film Festival (referred to as MLJFF) in Calgary, and COMMFFEST Global in Toronto are also long-running global film festivals that share a similar set of objectives: promoting cultural diversity, showcasing filmmakers from a variety of regions, and critically engaging with global issues. Other thematic film festivals curate films about specific global topics, such as those focusing on environmental issues such as conservation and climate change. The Environmental Film Festival, held annually in Washington, DC, since 1993, runs over 100 films hoping to encourage environmental activism. The We Art Water Film Festival is more narrowly focused, offering short films about the global clean water crisis. These film festivals often embrace a "green" ethos related to the environmental theme. For example, a cross section of films from the We Art Water Film Festival is made available through social networks, blunting the carbon footprint endured by traveling to the in-person festival.

At least two festivals draw awareness to world peace: the Global Peace Film Festival in Orlando and the Peace on Earth Film Festival in Chicago. The organizers of the Peace on Earth Film Festival hope their festival will "enlighten and empower individuals, families, and communities to step out of the ignorance of conflict, violence and divisiveness, into the light of communication, consideration, tolerance and understanding" (Peace on Earth Film Festival, 2014). Finally, migration is a global theme around which several film festivals have been organized. These festivals, such as the Immigration Film Fest and the Global Migration Film Festival, advertise themselves as celebrations of migrants and immigrants to the communities to which they have relocated. Since 2016, the Global Migration Film Festival has run in various cities from the end of November until International Migrants Day on December 18, for example. The Human Trafficking Awareness Day and Film Festival is more justice-oriented, aiming to disrupt patterns of sex trafficking by showcasing fiction and nonfiction films about human trafficking in the US and Western Europe.

Film festivals focused on human rights have enjoyed most scholarly attention among the various types within the broad genre of *global problems film festivals* (see de Jong & Bronkhorst, 2017; Grassilli, 2012; Tascón, 2012, 2015; Wils, 2017; Wong, 2011). The frequency of these examinations relative to the lack of studies on other global thematic film festivals is likely a result of the increased proliferation of human rights film festivals and discourse since the late 1980s. Since then, a robust network of human rights film festivals has developed, supported by human rights-oriented NGOs such as *People in Need* and *Amnesty International*. Most human rights film festivals draw inspiration from the Universal Declaration of Human Rights (UDHR), proclaimed by the United Nations General Assembly in 1948 (Grassilli, 2012). These festivals are typically dominated by documentaries, indicating an "epistemological predisposition to the documentary form" as a mode of purveying truth and bearing witness to the same (Wong, 2011, p. 173). This predisposition is in part owed to the relative cost of producing works of fiction; directors of documentaries are less beholden to box office concerns and, as a result, have greater latitude to choose topics for their films that may lack broad appeal. The privileging of documentaries, however, is also based on the assumption that these films are more educational and therefore better aligned with the purposes of the festival (Tascón, 2017a; Wong, 2011). Too, the documentary is often viewed as less subjective and more factual than fictional, narrative films and therefore carries an aura of trustworthiness that feature-length films lack (see Livingston, 2014; Marcus & Stoddard, 2009).

Perhaps the most visible and oldest human rights film festival is the Human Rights Watch Film Festival (HRWFF), which has run annually in New York and London while also moving to various other locations. Human Rights Watch launched this festival in 1988 on the fortieth anniversary of the signing of the UDHR. Since then, HRWFF has been curated such that selected films closely resonate with projects being undertaken by its parent organization. The stated goal of HRWFF is to "bear witness to human rights violations and create a forum for courageous individuals on both sides of the lens to empower audiences with the knowledge that personal commitment can make a difference" (Human Rights Watch Film Festival, 2018). The organizers of the HRWFF expect that the visual medium of film will inspire discourse and action around human rights abuses in ways unlikely through abstract statistics alone. John Biaggi, the director of HRWFF, argues, "Films bring an immediacy and an emotional level that reports do not. The visual medium is the arena where human rights can really be detailed and brought to an audience who can understand it on a personal level" (as cited in Wong, 2011, p. 175). However, Biaggi also emphasizes that HRWFF avoids films that are excessively graphic in their portrayals of human rights crimes or are overtly political in their message (Swimelar, 2010).

An intention of political neutrality in any global film festival is complicated by the construction and curation of these events for particular audiences, an arrangement structured by local and global power relations (Boltanski, 1999; Chouliaraki, 2006; Sontag, 2003; Tascón, 2012). One might contend, for example, that the very denotation of a *global* film festival has a political predisposition from the outset. Scholars who have theorized the relationship of spectator and image have concluded that viewing humanitarian films is not a neutral endeavor since attendees are privileged by their typically Western position as *saviors* and *viewers* while the subjects of films are positioned as *victims* and *viewed* (Tascón & Wils, 2017). This "humanitarian gaze" allows festival-goers to "look at others' troubles, with the expectation that the gaze will not be returned," retaining the "unequal relationship between gazer and gazed" (Tascón, 2017b, p. 75). The attendee remains distant from the suffering on the screen; the very act of viewing others' pain underscores the positionality of film festivals and their audiences. As a result, humanitarian film festivals risk reducing the subjects of films to "humanitarian objects," fixing them in their tragedy, and narrowing their agency (Tascón, 2015, 2017b). This tension echoes the previously noted criticism of global concerts being organized by those in the global North for audiences and with musicians from the same background.

A certain genre of film festivals, referred to as activist film festivals, have responded to the object-subject positionality problem inherent in the grammar of these events. Tascón and Wils (2017) observe potential in *activist film festivals*, which are platforms reaching "the 'heart' of the relations of power that contribute to the problem [examined by films in a particular festival], and attempt to change the conditions of its creation" (p. 6). Activist film festivals seek to disrupt the strict binary of attendee and film through pre- and post-screening activities involving complex debates and lively participation on the parts of attendees, in ways reflective of the "earn your way into the concert" app of Global Citizen (Iordanova, 2012). For example, post-screening discussions at activist film festivals are not the typical Q&A sessions where filmmakers and stars inform the audience about the film they have just viewed. Rather, these lengthy discussions are designed to help audiences move beyond the artistic expression and engage the social world of the issues portrayed in the film (Iordanova, 2012). Scholars have identified the Buenos Aires Human Rights Arts and Film Festival and the imagineNATIVE Film + Media Arts Festival in Toronto as film festivals embodying the ethos of collective participation (Tascón, 2017a; Thornley, 2017). To some degree, the participatory nature of all film festivals—from the employ of social media by attendees to the pop-up bazaars of locally resourced/globally conscious goods to the necessarily interpretive space opened up when watching a filmic rendering of an issue—attempts to undo the active/passive, gazed/gazer positionality inherent in this genre of global events.

Methods

In this chapter, we present data drawn from observations, interviews with attendees and organizers, and analyses of the programs and ephemera associated with two global film festivals: the UNAFF and the MLJFF. Our approach to data collection at the film festivals was organized in advance but mitigated by the on-the-ground circumstances of each event. In planning to attend, we read carefully the website and social media feeds for the events, identifying the films and related activities planned. We took notes on the websites to identify the stated purposes and contents of the festivals. We then attended the festivals as participants, viewing the films, sitting next to a diverse range of attendees over the course of the 3–5-day visits, doing brief on-site interviews with those who wished to engage in a conversation, and conducting more extensive interviews via digital video call with some participants as well as the organizers of the festivals. We took notes of pertinent observations *in situ* along with ideas and concerns raised by attendees while writing internal memos outlining key data points and working theories about the events. Prior to interviewing people on site, we provided them with our IRB human subjects participation forms and explained the study we were doing. An unintended consequence and benefit of this approach was that word circulated within the events of researchers studying participation in the festival which led to individuals seeking us out to give their input as well as connection-making with local individuals known in the community who were interested in the research we were undertaking. This unanticipated experience reminded us of the transient and affiliative community which these festivals create.

The Festivals

The UNAFF is an 11-day festival founded in 1998 by Jasmina Bojic and supported by the Stanford Film Society and the Midpeninsula Chapter of the United Nations Association. Its initial run was timed to recognize the fiftieth anniversary of the signing of the UN Declaration of Human Rights. Since its inception, the festival has been led by Bojic, a lecturer in international relations and director of the *Camera as Witness Program* at Stanford University. It is the longest-running global film festival in North America, occurring every October in Palo Alto, San Francisco, and at Stanford University. According to Bojic, a central aim of the festival is to use "documentary filmmaking as a tool for education and arts for social justice." Bojic aims to keep prices as low as possible: admission is free for students, while the general public pays $12 per session. Each session typically includes two short films, one full-length feature film, and a question-and-answer session with the filmmakers. The festival also includes free panel sessions with filmmakers and commentators on issues relevant to the festival.

The 2019 theme of UNAFF was Scales of Justice. According to Bojic, UNAFF strives to give a "cross-section of the world by illuminating numerous issues from various countries, bound together by the common thread of the Universal Declaration of Human Rights" (2012, para. 2). However, UNAFF has no official affiliation with the United Nations, and the UN Declaration of Human Rights gets little coverage in the promotional materials associated with the festival. Rather, UNAFF aims to be an early outlet for documentary films on timely global issues that will go on to a wider distribution. Sixty films total were shown (out of 600 submissions); some were full-length features (running between 50 minutes and two hours) and others were short films (between six and 25 minutes). UNAFF bestows six awards to films in the program: the UNAFF Grand Jury Award for Best Documentary, the UNAFF Grand Jury Award for Best Short Documentary, the UNAFF Youth Vision Award, the UNAFF Award for Cinematography, the UNAFF Award for Editing, and the UNAFF Visionary Award.

The MLJFF is a six-day Canadian documentary film festival, running annually in November.[1] It began in 2006 in the Marda Loop neighborhood of Calgary, the largest city in the western province of Alberta. Executive Director Jennifer Ewen notes that MLJFF was started by a group of educators who aimed to counteract the commercialization of Alberta with "an altruistic type of an event." Organizers saw the MLJFF as a way of educating a wider community about global events and activating those in the community already engaged in addressing peace, human rights, diversity, and ecological issues with the festival providing a wider frame to connect these discourses. Like UNAFF, the organizers of MLJFF aim for the greatest possible accessibility by making the event free to attendees. Also like UNAFF, the ethos of global citizenship is evident in MLJFF's program, website, and other ephemera. The MLJFF employs the motto *Good Films. Do Good.* to signal its intention of making the event a venue for planning future actions, as a global citizen might view these interactions. MLJFF is not a single-issue film festival as the unifying theme is a broad one focused on justice on a variety of social levels.

UNAFF and MLJFF offer informative case studies of global film festivals. Both efforts have expanded significantly throughout their respective existences, reaching a greater number of attendees and screening a larger number of documentaries each year. UNAFF was originally a three-day festival and now runs for 11 days while MLJFF began as a three-day festival and has grown to a six-day festival. Both festivals feature documentaries on global problems and advocate for action around these issues. They partner with local NGOs and nonprofits to host screenings and encourage immediate action in the local community while deepening the impact of those same organizations. Both festivals also offer year-round programming in schools and libraries in the hope of expanding conversations beyond the festival sessions. Consistent with other global film festivals, we noted at the sessions we observed that attendees tended to fall within three demographic categories, including being 40+ in age, white, and female (Roy, 2016). The demographics of the film festivals in comparison to concerts, especially with respect to attendee age, is quite interesting, given that the former appeals to those over 40 and the latter to those under 40. The divergences in format and execution between these festivals also allow for particular insights related to the contexts. MLJFF boasts a leaner program than UNAFF, running 19 films during the 2019 festival. As will be explored in detail below, although both festivals are affiliated with regional United Nations Associations, the organizers align their festivals with the mandate of the United Nations differently. But first, we offer an analysis of the distinct ways these festivals are shaped by their geographic contexts.

Insights

The Setting Shapes the Agenda

In choosing two globally oriented film festivals running in distinct geographic settings, we observed the ways in which the social–political contexts offered unique profiles for each event. While the context of any film festival is likely to shape its proceedings, this appears particularly acute at global film festivals. Mainstream film festivals that support big-budget movies are exclusive affairs, occurring in large theaters and ritzy ballrooms. In contrast, due to the optics of examining issues of global poverty and injustice in a humble setting coupled with a desire to keep the festivals as inexpensive, and thereby as accessible, as possible, the organizers of both festivals we observed integrated the proceedings into local community contexts in locations appropriate to explicitly public pedagogy, such as a university and a library. At UNAFF, films are screened in various community centers, a local middle and high school, and on Stanford University's campus. The MLJFF took place intentionally throughout Calgary, at various film houses and libraries, though the main venue was in a church located at the center of the neighborhood that bears the name of the festival. Thus, the constitution of global film festivals is potentially shaped to a greater degree by their contexts because of their reliance on local institutions, community-based organizations, and universities, serving to underscore the overtly public mission of the event.

Calgary is a western Canadian city that is known as the "energy city." Calgary sits geographically isolated from the politically dominant eastern provinces of Ontario and Quebec. Most notably, Calgary is a hub for petroleum investment; the city is known as a resource hub since every major producer and distributor in the oil industry is headquartered there. The province of Alberta, with its capital in Edmonton, produces 80% of all Canadian oil and shale gas as the province sits atop a massive deposit of oil sands. Given its status as the epicenter of oil capital, the politics of Calgary tends right on the political spectrum, though with a measure of "live and let live" ethos. To this point, most Calgarians—labeled "conservation conservatives"—support traditionally liberal causes such as the environment and gay marriage, though relative to the Eastern provinces, are more politically conservative (Elliott, 2015).

Palo Alto is another industry epicenter, but with a much different character than Calgary. Palo Alto is a key city in the Silicon Valley, home to major tech headquarters and Stanford University. Located in the San Francisco Bay Area, it is an intellectual-tech haven, with companies such as Apple, Google (now in Mountain View), Facebook (now Meta), Hewlett-Packard, Tesla, Skype, Lockheed Martin, and other technology giants headquartered in the Palo Alto region. Palo Alto is one of the most expensive cities in which to live in the US and its residents are among the most educated (Scheinin, 2016). The politics of Palo Alto skew liberal with over half of registered voters identifying as Democrats (Elections Division, 2019). While 60% of the permanent residents of Palo Alto are white (Metropolitan Transportation Commission, n.d.), Palo Alto is a cosmopolitan city, with a noticeable presence of international immigrants who come to study at Stanford University and/or work in one of its many tech firms.

The contexts these cities provide for each global film festival are in stark contrast. Calgary is politically right of center, relies heavily on a fossil fuel economy, and is moderately populated within a vast, rural expanse. Palo Alto is politically left of center, in a state that is among the most politically liberal in the US. It is future-focused on the tech sector and cutting-edge innovation and sits contiguous with one of the largest populations in the US—the Bay Area. These distinct backdrops shape the agenda of the global film festivals they host.

While both festivals attempt connections between global issues and what attendees can do locally through their off-screen events (explored in more detail later in this chapter), MLJFF seems to be more intentional in selecting films either by local filmmakers or that are centered on issues that are global in nature but deeply connected to western Canada. With a more limited program, this ethos of synthesizing the global intentions of the festival with issues significant to Alberta was present in MLJFF from its origins. In explaining its beginnings, MLJFF organizer Jennifer Ewen says:

> The main purpose [of the festival] is to increase awareness of variety of social environmental justice issues right here in Calgary... it started off 14 years ago with a group of teachers that felt that with all the oil money in this town, the amount of money being spent on entertainment events, that there was a space for something that had a little bit more, you know, an altruistic type of an event. The idea was to put on an event that wasn't just about making money and about entertainment or sport. That there would be a way to educate and increase awareness of some of these issues in Calgary.

A good illustration of this intention was a documentary film that profiled three Albertan women who were of Indian origin and were sexually abused as children by a family visitor in the 1980s. The universality of sexual abuse and the particularity of these Indian immigrants to Alberta demonstrates this principle in the design of the festival. This session, which included a discussion with the three women, was among the more powerful events of the MLJFF with overflow attendance and lengthy dialogue. The fact that the women reported the abuse by an Indian visitor—but in their Calgary home—made the narrative especially resonant as many of the attendees for this session were of south Asian descent. The dialogue was also carried off with a hint of nativism or xenophobia, which given the origins of the perpetrator of the abuse, one could imagine happening in other venues.

Though UNAFF does not dissociate itself from the immediate context, it appears more cosmopolitan in how it represents itself to attendees. UNAFF films were mainly cross-national collaborations, and the program itself advertises the international elements of the festival by identifying the national origins of the filmmakers in the program. Our read of the programs of both festivals suggests that UNAFF boasts a broader sampling of films from across the globe. In addition, UNAFF has a traveling film festival that partners with other United Nations Associations. This auxiliary effort occurs once a month for one or two days in cities such as New York, Los Angeles, Paris, and Abu Dhabi. MLJFF's auxiliary event, described in greater detail below, does not generally show films outside of Calgary. Finally, Bojic sees the mission of UNAFF to be a platform to launch global films into wider distribution. Past films screened at UNAFF, such as *How to Learn to Skateboard in a Warzone (If You're a Girl)*, have gone on to win Oscars, an accomplishment UNAFF is intentional about promoting in their social media posts. Thus, we observed an aim for a more global profile within UNAFF's efforts. One way of comparatively interpreting the festivals is that MLJFF brings the world to Calgary and UNAFF brings Palo Alto to the world.

The contrast between Canadian and US national contexts is significant here as well. Being globally connected and conversant is less salient and more obvious in Canada, as Canadians view themselves proportionally in-the-world in a way that Americans generally do not. The US has a stronger orientation toward viewing immigrants as foreigners, despite an immigrant legacy. Canada is also a nation of immigrants, though different in that the US expects assimilation by immigrants while Canada is more embracing of cultural pluralism, at least in a symbolic way. This, coupled with Canada's disposition in the world as *participant* as compared to *as hegemon* as in the case of the US, makes the global aspect of the film festival somewhat less special in Canada than it would be in California.

Attendees reacted to these agendas in ways that suggested particular challenges and possibilities, as organizers seek to strike the right balance between local contexts and the global themes of the films. Jennifer Ewen noted that MLJFF brought in higher-profile speakers for their off-screen events in 2019, relying less on local experts than in years past. Despite this attempt to develop conversations about the films that moved beyond the context of Calgary, as outsiders we found the local connections that structure MLJFF made it more difficult for non-locals to link with the events. There is always a local story that backdrops these global events, and visitors are not often up to speed on what is happening locally to catch all the references. The issues in Calgary in late 2019 were largely about the stalled construction of a gas pipeline, which was held up politically by the eastern provinces, notably by the provincial legislature in Quebec. This political issue was referred to many times, particularly in response to the Indigenous-focused films about whale research and Arctic drilling. Despite these knowledge gaps for certain groups of attendees, ourselves included, the local story gives specificity and texture to the otherwise broad and amorphous Sustainable Development Goals 2015–2030 (SDG 15–30) that frame MLJFF. As a result, the local connections between the films, off-screen events, and attendees allowed for potentially robust discussions about the content of the films and resonant local examples where issues manifest.

Attendees of UNAFF, on the other hand, noted the contrast between the themes of UNAFF and the particular context of Palo Alto. Bojic, in serving as the master of ceremonies at UNAFF, often referenced local happenings when introducing films and panels. In our interview, she described the evolution of UNAFF and her attempts to build a festival that both championed global causes while serving the local community. However, this revealed a tension between the themes from the films and the choice of Palo Alto as a host city, a tension noticed by several attendees. Terrie, a teacher from the Bay area, commented that the location of UNAFF was "interesting because when I think about the history of Palo Alto, I don't think of […] social justice activism. Yes, it's progressive but not as radical as, like, Oakland and San Francisco or Berkley."

In this regard, Palo Alto, a relatively wealthy community, might feel like a misfit to host films whose themes include refugee crises, social justice, and global poverty, particularly given the way that Big Tech is implicated in exacerbating global injustices (e.g., fair trade, e-waste, and mining of rare earths for production). Bojic is aware of this concern and notes a major achievement of UNAFF is expanding its screenings to East Palo Alto, a more economically challenged community. Bojic also suggests Palo Alto provides an audience of financially resourced, politically liberal attendees who, after finding inspiration in the films, will support NGOs working on these issues. But for Bojic and UNAFF, success is foremost measured through the dissemination of films that otherwise would not be shown in theaters or on streaming services. In our interview, Bojic noted the number of films that first screened at UNAFF, secured distribution deals, and went on to be nominated for and win top documentary film prizes. She acknowledged that the appeal of Palo Alto as a "rich city" was more likely to bring a broader audience to UNAFF, thus spreading awareness about global topics.

These varying contexts offer affordances and constraints in the ways organizers take up the charge of running a global film festival. UNAFF resembles an industry film festival to a greater degree than MLJFF, awarding prizes and working to bring the films that run in its program to broader audiences. That Palo Alto is a five-hour drive from Hollywood may play some role in these aspirations. As a result, UNAFF reaches a wider audience, though the extent to which attendees connect with the films and each other during festival events remains unclear. Though MLJFF has grown every year since its inception, its reach is more limited and it has a smaller feel, less oriented to the film industry and more to the community and its connections to social issues. Again, geography plays some part as Calgary is far removed from film industry centers in addition to being geographically isolated from other population centers of North America.

With this more limited scope, non-locals may have to work harder to engage with the events of the festival. MLJFF offers locals a chance to network with each other over global issues that resonate within their community.

Program as Curriculum

The films, of course, are the central element of these events. We see the program of each festival as the formal curriculum of the event, as compared to the enacted curriculum that we witnessed, setting an agenda or plan and raising questions about important global issues into dialogue. But, as will become clear, this curriculum is guided by the context of the festival in several key ways, not the least of which is the receptivity of the audience (see media reception overview, Chapter 1). First, we examine the origins of the films in each festival, and then we consider the topics portrayed by these films across both programs. We then focus on the ways in which the previously described contexts interact with the types of films that run in each program and the origins of these festivals. Finally, we consider attendees' responses to the films to get a sense of how they understand the curriculum of these festivals.

We offer three methodological notes about our content analysis of the programs of these festivals. As noted earlier, UNAFF publishes the nationality of the filmmakers in their program. MLJFF is not as intentional in naming the national origins of their films, and thus we had to infer from available information the origins of each film. This contrast alone offers some insights into the contrasting mindsets of organizers. In addition, UNAFF boasts a large number of films that are cross-national collaborative efforts, so up to four nationalities may be represented in a single film. Finally, UNAFF ran 60 films in 2019, while MLJFF ran 15 films, making one-to-one comparisons difficult. With these caveats in mind, we will explore the global profile of each festival.

We represent the global scope of the creators of each film festival's curricula in Table 4.1. The country of origin matters insofar as these are film festivals with global aims. At least for the 2019 runs of each festival, UNAFF boasts a more comprehensive global profile than MLJFF. The extent to which the organizers of a festival center geographically diverse voices is in part a reflection of their commitment to global and divergent perspectives. The legacy of the film festival and the accessibility of its location may also contribute to the composition of the program. The greater diversity in country of origin in UNAFF films, a celebrated feature of the festival given that they name those countries in their program, may in part be owed to the relative age and profile of UNAFF as compared to MLJFF, as well as to the relative ease of travel to the Bay Area as compared to Calgary.

It is not surprising that the films that run at MLJFF are primarily created by Canadian and American documentarians given its small size, geographic positioning, and MLJFF being a newer festival. However, UNAFF, despite its more sizable diversity and commitment to showcasing global filmmakers, is also

TABLE 4.1 Origins of the Documentary Films

Nation of Origin	MLJFF	UNAFF	Total
Africa	2	7	9
Australia and New Zealand	0	4	4
East Asia and the Pacific Rim	1	5	6
Europe	2	17	19
Latin America	0	5	5
Southwest Asia and North Africa	0	7	7
South Asia	1	3	4
US and Canada	12	38	50

dominated by films from the US, Canada, and Europe. This centering of voices from the Global North appears to be a vestige of the historical development of film festivals generally, as we noted in Chapter 2. We recognize that both festivals are in North America and filmmakers will run their documentaries where they have access. However, we see the systemic features of the film industry, especially access to funding to make documentaries, and the global system writ large in the prioritizing of documentaries from the Global North. In other words, the power imbalance between observer and observed so common in other global events such as concerts, is ever present in these programs where an explicit attempt to rectify this balance is stated. This is an issue of representation that we revisit in Chapter 6 (Tascón & Wils, 2017).

Both festivals ran films that centered on topics integral to global citizenship education (GCE; see Chapter 1). We observed notable divergences despite the accordance of content under the aegis of GCE. Table 4.2 presents the range of topics covered by the films in both festivals.[2] Points of emphasis for both festivals appeared to be films relating to civil and human rights, environmental issues, gender, healthcare, and political movements. The films selected at UNAFF suggest a stronger emphasis on artistic expressions around the world, prison reform (largely in the US), and migration. Reflecting its Albertan context, the films selected by MLJFF bring a stronger focus on environmental issues and consumption and no films about art, perhaps a contrast in class orientation of the two locations. In either case, this range of topics includes issues and perspectives that would not normally see coverage in the mainstream media. For instance, the documentary *Conviction*, which ran at MLJFF, was collaboratively produced by a team of documentarians, activists, and women incarcerated in Canadian jails.

The prevalent issues in these films cohere with SDG 15–30, as the festivals align themselves with the United Nations in various ways. Though the UN's UDHR was an inspiration in the founding of UNAFF, by 2019, the festival appears more symbolically connected to the UN, working in parallel toward similar goals. MLJFF is more intentional in directly connecting each of the

TABLE 4.2 Topics of the Documentary Films

Topic	MLJFF	UNAFF	Total
Arts	0	7	7
Civil and Human Rights	3	10	13
Domestic Violence	1	2	3
Economics and Consumerism	3	2	5
Education	0	2	2
Environmental Issues	4	10	14
Gender and Women's Rights	3	5	8
Health and Healthcare	2	4	6
LGBTQ+ Issues	1	2	3
Politics and Political Movements	5	7	12
Prison Reform	1	8	9
Race and Culture	1	5	6
Refugees and Migration	1	12	12
War and Peace	1	5	6
Welfare	1	1	2

films in its program to UN SDG 15–30. The MLJFF's website, for example, the 25-minute film *The Sacred Place Where Life Begins*, which examines the efforts of Indigenous peoples to protect an island in Alaska's Arctic Refuge from oil and gas development, is aligned with SDG 13, Climate Action, and SDG 15, Life on Land. In addition, at the introduction of each film, explicit reference to one or more of the 17 SDGs goals was announced. As a result, UN SDG 15–30 gave MLJFF a common language with which to connect the films and was more prominently featured than UNAFF. Here again is a contrast as the SDG 15–30 framework is less salient within a country that positions itself as a global hegemon than one that aims to act proportionately globally.

Each film festival applies a different structure to its program, which potentially modulates attendees' engagement with the themes of the festival. UNAFF's screenings were organized into sessions containing two or three films typically united around a particular theme. For instance, three films relating to war ran during Session 2: *Mosul after the War*, *Project Mosul*, and *Who Killed Lt. Van Dorn?*. The MLJFF program, with fewer films running, was not organized into sessions. Some days of the festival a single film ran on its own. On other days, films ran back-to-back and were connected by theme. For example, on the fourth night of MLJFF, *The Sacred Place Where Life Begins* and *The Whale and the Raven*, which both focus on the environment and Indigenous people, ran sequentially. At other times, a central theme was not evident, such as on the fifth day of MLJFF when *Exiled* and *The Need to GROW* ran consecutively. The former film examines political violence in Burma, and the latter focuses on sustainable farming practices.

FIGURE 4.1 SDG 15–30 Prominently Placed in Signage throughout the Marda Loop Justice Film Festival, 2019

Authors' image.

Choice is built into the format of these events. The idea is not that participants will view every film, but that they pick and choose which ones interest them most, a prominent feature of public pedagogy (see Chapter 1) generally and a confounding dimension for those producing such events. This structure invites attendees to engage with the films in a personalized way such that for each attendee the enacted curriculum of the festival is unique. This choice was a particular draw for Melissa and Leslie to attend UNAFF. Leslie noted how the range of documentaries at UNAFF allowed her to view documentaries about "subjects that either I'm interested in, want to know more about, or maybe the subjects that I don't know anything about." With UNAFF, the diversity of experiences will be broader than MLJFF, given the larger array of choices. On the other hand, organizers have the opportunity to put forward a more coherent message with a more limited program in the case of MLJFF, though an organization that cannot guarantee attendees will witness all aspects of the event.

We noted common themes across audience reactions to film content. Most attendees we interviewed described increased knowledge resulting from the films, contrasting their learning at the festivals with their typical news consumption. At MLJFF, Trina said, "It's not normal, like in Calgary, to be informed, to be in the know of what's happening outside in the developing world. I felt like this could be a timely information source that talks about issues around the world." Melissa responded to the films she viewed during UNAFF in a similar manner and reflected on the limits of her knowledge of world affairs, stating, "It made me realize that there's a lot more to it that I don't always read about if I don't choose to read more in depth about things." She continued:

> [UNAFF] opens avenues of thought for me that I may not actively pursue now by going to the library and getting a book on something. But the next time maybe I see an article about one of these topics, instead of just reading the headline and pass it by, I may have, it may have sparked enough interest in me or make me feel like oh I know a little something about this. I'm going to read more about this.

This increase in content knowledge is in line with the goals of the festivals. UNAFF is advertised with the slogan "Documentaries that will change your view of the world." But the previously described goals of the festival directors suggest more tangible and action-oriented results. While Melissa and Leslie, both UNAFF attendees, reported sharing their new knowledge with loved ones and neighbors, and another UNAFF attendee reported donating to a nonprofit organization connected with the film *Once Was Water*, many attendees with whom we spoke reported feeling overwhelmed by the content and lost on next steps.

The depressing nature of the content of many of the documentaries was a recurring theme in both the interviews and in our reflective comments during our observations. Roy (2016) notes that festival directors will try to balance content between challenging, big issues, and documentaries that offer solutions or offer more engaging presentations of those issues. One example of this during UNAFF was the documentary *Come and Take It*. This short documentary highlighted an anti-gun protest movement dubbed "Cocks Not Glocks," wherein college students carried dildos on the University of Texas campus in protest of a state law allowing gun owners to carry a concealed weapon on public college campuses. This film followed *The Last Prayer*, a short documentary focusing on the 2019 mass shootings at two mosques in Christchurch, New Zealand, and brought some levity to this particular session. Similarly, MLJFF featured a whimsical *Sex, Drugs and Bicycles* documentary of life in the Netherlands told from an outsider's perspective.

Still, attendees' and our responses to the festival suggest an engagement with affective elements of the content but feeling limited in taking action in response. In our field notes, we both reflected on the emotional toll we experienced as attendees ourselves. For instance, *One Child Nation*, which ran at MLJFF, was completely overwhelming to us and to many others in the audience.

The imagery of discarded babies in plastic bags thrown on trash heaps was searing and caused audible gasps, as did the sheer scale of the atrocities. Trina described the nightmares she experienced after viewing *One Child Nation* due to its "traumatic" and "intense" imagery. Leslie struggled with how she felt after viewing the UNAFF films, remarking, "It is entertainment and it's very thought provoking, but it's not like you come out with a particularly positive attitude after a lot of these films. It's pretty depressing."

Auxiliary Events—Less Viewing, More Doing

Bojic is aware of how taxing these documentaries can be on attendees, often using auxiliary events as a forum for discussing what might be done in response to the documentaries. Our interviews, observations, and the extant literature on human rights film festivals suggest these auxiliary events are as important to attendees as the films themselves (Czach, 2010; Davies, 2017).[3] Auxiliary events aim to bring together various stakeholders—filmmakers, activists, and local community members—to provide an informal place to discuss the global issues raised by the films. We observed informal learning environments that mixed film and education to produce a relaxed atmosphere for exchanging ideas, reactions, and information. These auxiliary events represent a smaller time commitment than reading a book or taking a class while holding the potential for learning and inspiration around topics with which attendees might not normally engage.

The organizers of MLJFF and UNAFF plan events both year-round and during the festivals to generate and sustain interaction, deepen awareness, and inspire action around issues related to the films. *justREEL* is an outgrowth of MLJFF and screens one feature film in January, March, May, and September, building toward the larger event in October. In light of the COVID-19 health crisis, the 2020 *justREEL* film screenings moved online, with volunteers recommending documentaries thematically linked to upcoming events, such as World Refugee Day and National Indigenous History Month. MLJFF also moved to be online in November 2020 and organizers subsequently changed the festival name to Calgary Justice Film Festival. These documentaries are widely available on streaming services like Netflix and YouTube, thus bypassing the submission-selection process typical of film festivals. Similarly, UNAFF's work extends beyond the festival in October, encompassing a robust network of global film programs throughout the year. Several programs, such as *UNAFF and Kids* and *UNAFF in Schools*, aim to engage younger audiences in documentaries on global topics, while others, such as *UNAFF for Seniors*, are aimed at older audiences. Like MLJFF, UNAFF also moved to virtual programming in response to the COVID-19 crisis, screening films and hosting question-and-answer panels with filmmakers over the video conferencing platform Zoom.

Besides the festival itself, MLJFF organizes an auxiliary event titled Peace Village. This is a partnership with a local NGO whose mission is advocacy for sustainable peace and minimization of military conflicts through education. Peace Village is an informational fair and international marketplace where attendees are expected to have discussions about the issues in the films and sample a variety of local and international food. Peace Village offered an opportunity for local artisans to share their projects and sell related objects. Jennifer Ewen remarked on the purpose of Peace Village to draw attendees' attention toward "sustainability and ethically produced products," though she went on to note that the event has become broader than perhaps initially envisioned. We observed a tension between the responsible consumerism at the root of Peace Village and the action called for by many of the films. For instance, at Peace Village Nepalese women who were exploited and in recovery sold handmade jewelry alongside more overtly political organizations, such as the group fighting in defense of Palestine. For attendees, the value is to view what is being done to tangibly address issues raised in the films. There was a sense of hope in these actions, while giving these entrepreneurs an opportunity to sell their merchandise. However, the strong economic focus potentially crowds out the non-economic imperatives of the work called for through the films while failing to recognize that commerce alone will not solve endemic global problems such as the plight of Palestinians in Israel.

Peace Village operates almost as an independent event parallel with MLJFF; it runs concurrently with the festival and is grounded on the same ethos, but does not make direct connections to the films themselves. One might conceivably attend Peace Village without viewing any of the films at MLJFF. The principal auxiliary events at both festivals, however, are the informal spaces for attendees to discuss the films with filmmakers, content area experts, and each other immediately following the screenings. Throughout the UNAFF program are community forums related to the themes of the films. The seventh session of UNAFF featured three films investigating different aspects of migration and the challenges of resettling refugees. UNAFF hosted a panel titled "Rights and Responsibilities" in the same venue where the films were shown immediately following this session. At post-screening discussions, we observed the filmmakers, and in several cases, the individuals at the center of the documentaries, bring insights into the filmmaking process as well as the issues explored by the films.

Bojic said these discussions allow "the subject of the film, filmmakers, experts, and the community to get together and create a space of awareness and empathy." Ewen noted she has received "a lot of feedback about how much people enjoyed talking to the people that were actually involved in creating the films and being in the film." There is an emotional element to these discussions, one that would be difficult to replicate by simply viewing the documentaries. For instance, following the screening of *The Last Prayer*, producer and director Ali Mustafa spoke on the emotional toll he endured making this documentary. His voice broke and he appeared to have tears in his eyes and he described his interviews with survivors and loved ones of those murdered. There were also joyful moments. The talkback following *Because We Are Girls* involved the subjects of the film—three sisters who had been sexually abused by a family member—and the filmmaker. While watching these women confront their parents on their failure to protect them was extremely upsetting, hearing them talk about their understanding and forgiveness for their parents was uplifting. These speakers received multiple standing ovations and others likely felt as we did: a desire to symbolically appreciate their courage and trauma by standing and cheering. This is one of the important value-adds to these events—appealing to people's basic humanity through incredibly powerful stories of struggle, survival, loss, and hope.

Post-viewing discussions such as these were identified by attendees as the most striking moments from both festivals, with attendees speaking as often about these moments as they did the films themselves. What they felt they gained from these experiences was somewhat varied. Some spoke of being better prepared to take action on issues relating to the themes of the festivals. Jules, an attendee of UNAFF, reported gaining insights into "how to be true to our conscience and change the world with it" after a question-and-answer session with Joseph Stillman, the director of *Citizen Clark*, a documentary about former US Attorney General Ramsey Clark's advocacy of human rights and criticism of the US as a plutocracy based solely on economic interests and avarice. More commonly, attendees spoke about connecting with the filmmakers themselves, rather than engagement with the issues of the films. Leslie, who attended several UNAFF sessions, said the auxiliary events brought viewing the documentaries "full circle," while Melissa, another UNAFF attendee, was reminded of "how much goes into making a movie that might only be 60 or 70 minutes long." Terrie, a third UNAFF attendee, spoke one-on-one with one of the subjects of the film *Broken Places* and offered her critique of how the filmmakers portrayed the subject's story.

These auxiliary events are memorable for their potential to deepen the knowledge attendees gain from the documentaries and to create an experience where attendees are brought closer to the films, their makers, and their subjects. There also appears to be a social aspect of these events that is unique from the justice-oriented mission of these festivals. During our observations, we gained the sense there is a core group of people who participate every year, either as volunteers, audience members, or both. During auxiliary events, there was a palpable sense of comradery among many participants about the mission of the festivals and the power of documentary films to affect change. The enthusiasm emanating from the auxiliary events largely waned by the time we interviewed attendees several weeks after the festivals concluded, however. As Davies (2017) argues, face-to-face encounters where attendees can better understand the filmmakers' intentions are an important precondition for film festivals that aspire to sustained action toward global change. These auxiliary events certainly move these events beyond simple screenings, and the potential for a more transformative experience is there, but much of that potential appears untapped. In our concluding section, we theorize why.

Conclusions

Global activism resulting from these film festivals appears to be limited to learning more about particular issues, sharing information and articles with loved ones and community members, and funding or donating to nonprofit organizations. The attendees' responses implicitly acknowledge that watching documentaries is a passive event. Some attendees' responses also appeared to acknowledge the power imbalance at work, as they viewed the suffering of other people. In the curricula of film festivals, those people were usually located in the Global South, fixed in their tragedy (Tascón, 2015, 2017a). This is broadly consistent with other film festival research that suggests connecting observable action to documentaries is difficult; people often feel moved by documentaries but cannot describe tangible results (Gaines, 1999, p. 85). It is difficult to say to what extent these festivals help sustain commitments to global causes.

We do not mean to suggest that global film festivals must result in dramatic political reform to be considered successful. Davies (2017) warns against such an instrumental presumption and reminds us to not assume attendees are tapped into global political networks. Measuring learning outcomes is elusive, as documentary film festivals, especially those that are justice-oriented, are complex sites of public pedagogy that are not reducible to fixed objectives nor engaged with systematic assessment of learning. Even during a shorter festival like MLJFF, there is a great deal of content around demanding topics that may often be remote to attendees. The more films one views, it would seem the potential to experience compassion fatigue increases (Moeller, 1999). However, none of the attendees with whom we spoke expressed a lessening of their commitment to global problems, nor did any appear to attend out of a desire to voyeuristically watch others suffer. And an interesting contrast to note—unlike the concerts wherein some of the attendees were there just for the music and did not like the messaging around the event, no one expressed those sentiments in relation to UNAFF or MLJFF. The attendees of UNAFF and MLJFF, and likely attendees of other global film festivals, already find themselves committed to the causes of these documentaries. They attend because they feel compassion and want to learn more about pressing global issues while expressing an affiliation desire to connect with like-minded people.

What distinguishes global film festivals from other film festivals is the potential to build collective action around an issue, even if that collective action does not rise to the level of legislative or social change. The auxiliary events are moments where attendees can negotiate and name their positions on global issues. As such, we argue more attention must be paid to the timing and structure of the auxiliary events. Some attendees, while praising the auxiliary events, also commented on the limited opportunities they had to unpack the more difficult moments of the documentaries they viewed. We wondered if the areas of untapped potential in the auxiliary events were owed to the commercial nature of marketplaces like Peace Village. These events were focused more on conscious consumerism rather than education for systemic changes around the root causes of the issues depicted in the films.

The auxiliary events we observed tended to occur immediately after viewing films. They were limited to question-and-answer sessions, and at times felt rushed. We believe this is a greater potential for transformative experiences if the attendees are able to engage with the content of the films in a deeper and more prolonged manner. This might be done through pre-screening activities. We could envision festivals sharing links to recommended readings in their online programs and having attendees meet to discuss issues raised in the readings before viewing the films or perhaps engaging in a participatory activity that deepens understanding about an issue. These pre-screening activities would both intellectually and emotionally prepare attendees to view the films. Festivals might also pause films during their screenings to encourage dialogue throughout the evening, rather than relegating these discussions to immediately after the screening. Finally, we recommend the organizers consider ways to use social networks to sustain the connections made during the screenings. Organizers might develop book clubs or other social activities during the auxiliary events of the central festivals and integrate those newly formed networks into their year-round auxiliary events such as *justREEL* and *UNAFF in Schools* programs. These could also be extended to nearby schools, colleges, and universities as a means of extending the educational mission of the festivals.

What is clear from these two events, especially apparent now in the era of COVID-19, is how meanings surrounding global issues take life in a social event such as a film festival. The level of audience engagement, the rapt attention to speakers, the emotion and reactions of audiences to the viewing experience, and the purposeful mingling created by auxiliary events, all of it contribute to a memorable and signifying moment in an age of events. The interruption of ordinary time signaled by events like these creates space for participants, organizers, and documentarians alike to create a shared learning experience whose educative potential extends far beyond the time horizon of the event itself.

Notes

1 In 2021 the festival organizers renamed the event the Calgary Justice Film Festival. In this chapter we refer to the event as it was named when we collected our data.
2 These codes emerged inductively from our read of the programs.
3 Scholars of film festivals have used a variety of terms to refer to these features of film festivals: Davies (2017) calls them "off-screen" events, while Schwartz (2007) has described them as "extra-cinematic" and "para-cinematic" events. We have chosen to

use the term "auxiliary" events to differentiate the work of this book, which attempts to understand the global film festival through the lens of educational theory, from the work of cinema scholars, critics, and documentarians.

References

Bojic, J. (2012). *Support.* United Nations Film Festival. Retrieved December 13, 2021, from http://www.unaff.org/2012/support.html

Boltanski, L. (1999). *Distant suffering: Morality, media and politics* (1st ed.). Cambridge University Press.

Chouliaraki, L. (2006). *The spectatorship of suffering.* SAGE.

Czach, L. (2010). Cinephilia, stars, and film festivals. *Cinema Journal, 49*(2), 139–145.

Davies, L. (2017). Off-screen activism and the documentary film screening. In S. M. Tascón & T. Wils (Eds.), *Activist film festivals: Towards a political subject* (pp. 39–58). Intellect.

de Jong, M., & Bronkhorst, D. (2017). Human rights film festivals: Different approaches to change the world. In S. M. Tascón & T. Wils (Eds.), *Activist film festivals: Towards a political subject* (pp. 105–120). Intellect.

Elections Division. (2019). *Report of registration as of February 10, 2019: Registration by political subdivision by county.* California Secretary of State. https://elections.cdn.sos.ca.gov/ror/ror-odd-year-2019/politicalsub.pdf

Elliott, S. (2015, December 19). Calgary is conservative all right but not the way you might think. *CBC News.* https://www.cbc.ca/news/canada/calgary/calgary-politics-susan-elliott-column-1.3369960

Gaines, J. M. (1999). Political mimesis. In J. M. Gaines & M. Renov (Eds.), *Collecting visible evidence* (pp. 84–102). University of Minnesota Press.

Grassilli, M. (2012). Human rights film festivals: Global/local networks for advocacy. In D. Iordanova & L. Torchin (Eds.), *Film festival yearbook 4: Film festivals and activism* (pp. 31–47). St. Andrews Film Studies.

Human Rights Watch Film Festival. (2018). *About.* Retrieved December 13, 2021, from https://ff.hrw.org/about

Iordanova, D. (2012). Film festivals and dissent: Can film change the world? In D. Iordanova & L. Torchin (Eds.), *Film festival yearbook 4: Film festivals and activism* (pp. 13–30). St. Andrews Film Studies.

Livingston, E. M. (2014). *Representing documentary film in the social studies classroom: Lessons from an online professional development course* (Publication No. 3621783) [Doctoral dissertation, Teachers College, Columbia University]. ProQuest Dissertations Publishing.

Marcus, A. S., & Stoddard, J. D. (2009). The inconvenient truth about teaching history with documentary film: Strategies for presenting multiple perspectives and teaching controversial issues. *The Social Studies, 100*(6): 279–284.

Metropolitan Transportation Commission. (n.d.) *Bay Area Census: City of Palo Alto.* MTC-ABAG Library. http://www.bayareacensus.ca.gov/cities/PaloAlto.htm

Moeller, S. D. (1999). *Compassion fatigue: How the media sell disease, famine, war, and death.* Routledge.

Montreal World Film Festival. (n.d.). *Montreal world film festival.* Retrieved June 24, 2019, from http://www.ffm-montreal.org/en/informations.html

Muller, C. (2012). Human rights film festivals and human rights education: The Human Rights Arts and Film Festival (HRAFF), Australia. In D. Iordanova & L. Torchin (Eds.), *Film festival yearbook 4: Film festivals and activism* (pp. 165–173). St. Andrews Film Studies.

Peace on Earth Film Festival. (2014). *Who we are.* Retrieved December 13, 2021, from http://www.agnt.org/Film-Fest/poeff.html

Piekarczyk, K. (2015). Ware a making a change, don't forget: Introduction. In H. Kulhánková, M. de Jong, M. Carrión, & R. Bowles Eagle (Eds.), *Setting up a human rights film festival* (Vol. 2, pp. 5–16). Human Rights Film Network.

Roy, C. (2016). *Documentary film festivals: Transformative learning, community building & solidarity.* Sense Publishers.

Scheinin, R. (2016, March 29). Palo Alto, Atherton crack top 10 priciest ZIP codes in U.S. *San Jose Mercury News.* https://www.mercurynews.com/2016/03/29/palo-alto-atherton-crack-top-10-priciest-zip-codes-in-u-s/

Schwartz, V. R. (2007). *It's so French! Hollywood, Paris, and the making of cosmopolitan French film culture.* University of Chicago Press.

Sontag, S. (2003). *Regarding the pain of others* (1st ed.). Farrar, Straus and Giroux.

Swimelar, S. (2010). *Human rights through film: An essay and review of selected films from the human rights watch 2009 film festival.* The Johns Hopkins University Press. doi:10.1353/hrq.2010.0025

Tascón, S. M. (2012). Considering human rights films, representation, and ethics: Whose face? *Human Rights Quarterly, 34*(3), 864–883. doi:10.1353/hrq.2012.0057

Tascón, S. M. (2015). *Human rights film festivals: Activism in context.* Palgrave Macmillan.

Tascón, S. M. (2017a). Watching others' troubles: Revisiting "the film act" and spectatorship in activist film festivals. In S. M. Tascón & T. Wils (Eds.), *Activist film festivals: Towards a political subject* (pp. 21–38). Intellect.

Tascón, S. M. (2017b). 'The humanitarian gaze': Human rights films and glocalised social work. In M. Livholts & L. Bryant (Eds.), *Social work in a glocalised world* (pp. 71–86). Routledge. doi:10.4324/9781315628417

Tascón, S. M., & Wils, T. (Eds.). (2017). *Activist film festivals: Towards a political subject.* Intellect.

Thornley, D. (2017). imagineNATIVE film + media arts festival: Collaborative criticism through curatorship. In S. M. Tascón & T. Wils (Eds.), *Activist film festivals: Towards a political subject* (pp. 199–212). Intellect.

Wils, T. (2017). Refusal to know the place of human rights: Dissensus and the human rights arts and film festival. In S. M. Tascón & T. Wils (Eds.), *Activist film festivals: Towards a political subject* (pp. 121–138). Intellect.

Wong, C. H. (2011). *Film festivals.* Rutgers University Press.

5

AT-HOME EVENTS

Global Engagement in the Twenty-First Century?

Digital technologies have increasingly allowed for the consumption of content and interaction with others near and far. Social network sites such as Facebook, Twitter, and Instagram provide platforms for individuals to view, share, analyze, and discuss with others all manner of content. The possibilities provided by digital technologies allow for participation in a global system unknown to previous generations (boyd & Ellison, 2007; Jenkins, 2006; Miller et al., 2016). Once, televised concerts or film festivals would be texts consumed by viewers and attendees alone. Now, social network sites have become spaces for the constructions and performances of users' identities, making them fora for interactions about televised programs and online videos, reaching audiences far beyond those present for the event (Williams & Zenger, 2012). The COVID-19 pandemic, which required all manner of formerly face-to-face contact to occur in the online world, has only normalized interactivity over digital spaces. While online interactions might have once been considered "virtual" or "distanced," the extent to which social networking has been embedded in the day-to-day activities of average citizens challenges these descriptors.

Recognizing this new reality, event organizers have sought to leverage the communicative and interactional power of social networks. In some cases, in-person global events are augmented by digital offerings for would-be attendees unable to physically be present. In Chapter 3, we offered a treatment of how presenters during the Global Citizen concerts urged attendees to use Twitter to pressure world leaders and philanthropists to act on pressing issues, while Instagram became a venue for performative acts of global citizenship by attendees of these concerts. In this chapter, we bring our lens of analysis to what we are calling at-home events. We focus on two types of at-home events. One involves the sharing of user-created content and particular hashtags

DOI: 10.4324/9780429281570-5

on social networks to compel action around a particular global issue. The other type of event is at-home concerts, where attendees livestream pre-recorded performances and other content over the internet and are meant to interact simultaneously over social networks. We seek to explore how these events begin and function during their lifespan. By naming these moments as events, rather than movements—as is the case in the literature on liberation technology—we bound them with definitive beginnings and ends, though perhaps not without legacies as enduring as primarily in-person events. This chapter helps develop a broader understanding of the nexus of GCE and social networks.

Global Engagement in the Digital Age

Over the last 20 years, a broad array of scholarship has emerged on a variety of topics related to social network sites, including identity development, network analysis, privacy, impact on face-to-face relationships, and use of social network sites in schools and universities (boyd & Ellison, 2007). Reflective of the novelty of social networks, however, research into the ways in which they shape or are used in GCE and public pedagogy is currently limited. In this chapter, we aim to contribute to this literature by framing the use of social network events to inform and organize around global issues as global social network events. Much of the literature most closely related to our focus conceptualize political action through social network sites as a form of liberation technology, given that these platforms allow "citizens to report news, expose wrong-doing, express opinions, mobilize protest, monitor elections, scrutinize government, deepen participation, and expand the horizons of freedom" (Diamond, 2010, p. 70).

Lance Bennett (2003) theorized the possibilities for social networks to empower activists to make social change, writing just before the inception of Facebook, YouTube, and Twitter. Using a handful of examples of social network activism in 2003, such as the use of online platforms to organize in-person protests against Starbucks coffee shops, Bennett argued that the fluid, open, and decentralized nature of social networks allowed for broader, less ideologically driven coalitions for political and social change. Network analysis of recruitment patterns on Twitter relating to protests in 2011 in Spain in response to the financial crisis generally confirms this assumption. High-profile users trigger chains of tweets at higher magnitudes than ordinary users, but content is generally spread randomly throughout a network of loose coalitions made up of politically engaged users (González-Bailón et al., 2011).

One scholar has characterized these instantaneous exchanges of ideas and information among people across the globe as an "interactive direct democracy" (Gerbaudo, 2014, p. 85). Starting in 2009, the inspiration and support afforded popular uprisings in Moldova, Iran, Tunisia, Egypt, Libya, Belarus, Columbia, and other nations by Twitter and Facebook appeared to have borne out this potential. The integration of social networks into these direct actions is reflective of a frustration with governments, NGOs, and other organizations to find solutions to these issues (Bennett, 2003). Participants in direct actions against oppressive governments have reported to researchers that their use of social networks was an essential—though not the only—means for organizing in-person action, distributing information amongst members of a coalition, and voicing frustrations (Harlow, 2012; Salem, 2014; Zeb et al., 2016). These results suggest social networks provide global citizens with a powerful conduit to effect political and social change.

Initial news media analyses of the mass protests of the 2009 parliamentary elections in Iran framed this and other direct actions as "Twitter Revolutions," though scholarly analyses have tempered this narrative. Harlow (2012) and Salem (2014) offer the caveat to their findings that the social network applications their participants identified in inspiring and organizing direct actions appear less helpful in political organizing and making long-term changes. Empirical research into the case of Iran has suggested similarly that Twitter's role in the popular uprising has likely been overstated (Esfandiari, 2010; Gaffney, 2010; Wojcieszak & Smith, 2014). For example, Wojcieszak and Smith (2014) surveyed 2,800 young and educated Iranians a year after the 2009 elections and protests. While the internet was the most cited news source, Twitter was the least prevalent source of news for participants. A majority of respondents reported using social networks to discuss personal issues, rather than political and social issues. While this research suggests Iranians were more likely to use social networks for personal interactions than political mobilization, the authors also found that "social networking, commenting on blogs, and sending texts positively predicted internal efficacy," or increased their political understanding (p. 104).

The liberation technology perspective assumes technology is an inherently democratic tool, or at worst neutral in the struggle for social change. When formulating foreign aid efforts at encouraging sociopolitical change vis-à-vis internet activism, governments have essentially ignored or written off as aberrations where technology has been a tool for oppressive regimes (Christensen, 2011). Scholars have observed, however, the ways in which authoritarian governments have increasingly used social networks in savvy ways to further their own agendas and keep track of dissident movements (Christensen, 2011; Esfandiari, 2010; Giroux, 2009; Morozov, 2011; Poell, 2014). Perhaps most disconcerting is that social networks have also been used by racist and hate groups to recruit and organize around their political goals. Social networks have been "particularly effective for giving visibility and potentially constructing an aura of 'righteousness' in fascist practices and discourses" (Kompatsiaris & Mylonas, 2014, p. 110). Social networks *can* liberate, but they can also serve as a conduit toward legitimacy for Nazis and other extremist political groups who would seek to intimidate or purge peoples they deem unworthy of equal political and social status.

Digital Age Global Events

The literature reviewed in the previous sections leaves us with an inconclusive image of the role of social networks in influencing global, sociopolitical change. Much of the theoretical literature is optimistic, while empirical studies leave us with questions. It appears that social networks encourage political self-efficacy, however, even if it is not accompanied by lasting structural change. Global humanitarian groups are banking on social networks to provide them with a set of tools for setting agendas and informing broad audiences about issues (Thrall et al., 2014). Hugh Evans, CEO of Global Citizen, commented on these potentials in 2020, saying:

> The greatest progression is the digital evolution of activism — how it has blossomed in the last 10 years due to the power of connectivity through Twitter, Instagram and other social network platforms that we are on, heavily, as well as YouTube. It is more possible to bring the world together faster. I couldn't imagine, 10 years ago, that we could be broadcast into 180 countries as was "Global Goals" this weekend. When Miley Cyrus and Coldplay tweeted at the Prime Minister of Sweden, and he replies that his country will step up its investment in developing and distributing vaccines, it's amazing to see the confluence of pop and public policy all at once.
>
> *(Amorosi, 2020)*

In the following sections, we examine the life cycles of four at-home events. All four events occurred over social network sites. Two of them involve a heavy reliance on hashtags and user sharing and liking. As noted in Chapter 2, hashtags are a tool embedded in social network sites, primarily Twitter, for linking posts related to a particular topic. From an operative perspective, hashtags allow users to quickly find posts about a topic. Hashtags also "simultaneously function semiotically by marking the intended significance of an utterance" (Bonilla & Rosa, 2015, p. 5). In other words, hashtags signal to users a position on an issue, "marking texts as being 'about' a particular topic" (Bonilla & Rosa, 2015, p. 5). In this chapter, we refer to these events as "global hashtag events." The other events also engage with social network interactivity while broadcasting musical performances and documentaries through social network platforms. We begin our analysis with the global hashtag events.

Global Hashtag Events

Kony 2012

Kony 2012 was a viral campaign fueled by a 30-minute documentary by the same name. In this chapter, when referring to the documentary *Kony 2012*, we italicize the title. When the term "Kony 2012" is not italicized, we are referring to the broader campaign. A cultural phenomenon prompting immediate and widespread response, Kony 2012 highlights the potentials and limitations of using social networks for affecting global civic action. The documentary was produced and distributed by Invisible Children, an NGO founded in 2004 by three American college students: Jason Russell, Bobby Bailey, and Laren Poole. While filming a documentary about the War in Darfur in 2003, the trio became aware of the Lord's Resistance Army (LRA), a Christian terrorist group operating in Central Africa led by warlord Joseph Kony. Kony and the LRA committed all manner of atrocities, including abducting children who were used as soldiers and sex slaves, crimes for which Kony was indicted in 2005 by the International Criminal Court.

Invisible Children made exposing the crimes perpetrated by Kony and the LRA to a broader audience its *raison d'être*, with much of its efforts going toward producing documentary films while also conducting on-the-ground humanitarian operations in Central Africa (Brough, 2012). Their campaigns were typically two-pronged, relying on both social network sharing and on-the-ground, grassroots organizing. *Kony 2012* would be the 11th documentary Invisible Children produced and distributed through social network sites like Facebook and Twitter, as well as clubs on college campuses and places of worship (Karlin & Matthew, 2012). When US president Barack Obama signed the "Lord's Resistance Army Disarmament and Northern Uganda Recovery Act" in 2010, he referenced the documentary and social network efforts of Invisible Children as influential in generating bipartisan support for an American response to the crimes of Kony and the LRA (Rozen, 2012). Thus by early 2012, Invisible Children had a well-established network of supporters sharing their content, including celebrities and policymakers.

Kony 2012 is both the origin story of Invisible Children and a call to action. Narrated by Invisible Children co-founder Jason Russell, the documentary is as much an autobiographical story about Russell and his relationship to the conflict in Central Africa, as it is about Kony and his crimes. It is a well-produced documentary, employing quick edits and emotional imagery. Watching it ten years later, even knowing the short-lived impact the film would have, we were struck by how powerful certain elements of the film could be. After a brief introduction (which we describe below), the documentary begins with Russell expressing his desire for his son Gavin to live in a better world than the one he was born into. Russell describes Kony's crimes to Gavin, a telegenic young boy the same age as many of the LRA's victims. Ostensibly, Gavin is an avatar for the viewers of the documentary; as Russell explains in simple terms what makes Kony "the bad guy," he is also educating an unaware American and European audience. This sequence springboards into a brutal presentation of LRA's crimes, with photographs and videos of mutilated faces and bodies. The viewers also meet Jacob, a Ugandan victim of the LRA who Russell befriended while filming in Africa. Jacob, whose brother was murdered by the LRA, breaks down in tears trying to describe what he would say to his brother if he were to see him again. Russell makes a promise to Jacob to dedicate his life to stopping the LRA and bringing Kony to justice.

Russell transitions to recounting the work of Invisible Children as his effort to keep that promise. The logic of *Kony 2012* and Invisible Children's other efforts is that if only ordinary people knew about Kony's crimes, they would pressure powerful governments to intervene. Awareness leads naturally to action. *Kony 2012* concludes by announcing the "Cover the Night" campaign, an effort to make Kony famous. Russell asks viewers to tweet at a specific group of 20 celebrities, athletes, and billionaires, asking these influential people to share information about Kony and the LRA on their social network sites. Russell also asks viewers to contact 12 policymakers using tools on the Invisible Children website. The second part of the Cover the Night campaign involved in-person action on April 20, 2012, when committed activists would hang Kony 2012 posters, stickers, and signs in their local communities. Viewers were encouraged to purchase an "action kit" with a t-shirt, signs, stickers, bracelets, etc., branded with the stylized "Kony 2012" logo.

The Kony 2012 campaign was massively popular, though quickly became a lightning rod for criticism. Soon after its release, some commentators wondered if Invisible Children had invented a new model for global humanitarian activism (Holligan, 2012). The documentary was initially a mega success with 40 million views on YouTube after one week, and it was a top-10 trending topic on Twitter the week the video was released. At the time of writing, the video has over 100 million views—the fastest video on YouTube to reach that mark (Kanczula, 2012)—and 1.3 million "likes" on the video-sharing site (Invisible Children, 2012). There were also 3.6 million pledges of support to the Kony 2012 campaign. Officials from the International Criminal Court, UNICEF, and the United States Holocaust Memorial Museum praised the documentary, while retweets and shares from celebrities such as Justin Bieber, Rihanna, and Oprah appear to have driven popular attention (Kanczula, 2012). However, the pendulum quickly swung the other way. Critics accused the documentary of oversimplifying a longstanding and complicated conflict (Okwonga, 2012) and of misrepresenting Kony's location and the strength of LRA forces (Greenblatt, 2012; Keating, 2012), with some critics suggesting that energy would be better spent helping the victims of Kony's crimes rather than focusing on Kony himself (Mollins, 2012). The Cover the Night event in April of 2012 failed to generate much in-person activism (Miller, 2012). The long-term impact of the Kony 2012 campaign may also have been impacted by Russell's public breakdown, brought on by the stress of the sudden fame he received. A video of Russell's breakdown also went viral, leading to cruel spoof videos which deflated the momentum propelling the campaign (Bal et al., 2013; Harris, 2012).

Despite its sudden rise and fall, the Kony 2012 campaign was notable as a global event. It was episodic and participatory, centering around youthful engagement with a media artifact. Much like the Global Citizen concerts examined in Chapter 3, Invisible Children hedged its efforts on tapping into a young audience eager to use Web 2.0 and mobile technologies to empower global citizens to engage in connective action via personalized social networks (Chazal & Pocrnic, 2016; Karlin & Matthew, 2012). For instance, though the subject of the documentary is war crimes in Central Africa, its introduction focuses exclusively on the potential of social networks to remake the world. Africa is not even mentioned until four minutes into the 30-minute documentary. Rather, in the opening line, Russell says, "Right now, there are more people on Facebook than there were on the planet 200 years ago" (0:24). Footage of the Arab Spring protests is set next to flashes of comments under a YouTube video, while Russell says, "governments are trying to keep up, and older generations are scared" (1:18). Other portions of the documentary similarly take place on the narrator's Facebook timeline; as Russell describes actions Invisible Children has taken to thwart the LRA, the screen flashes from video-to-video embedded in an imaginary Facebook timeline. In other words, Kony 2012 makes the argument for global citizenship as enacted through social networks. Thanks to social networks, the world is, finally, truly flat (Freidman, 2006).

Much like the traditional face-to-face events, the Kony 2012 campaign also relied on familiar tropes of emotive storytelling, distant suffering, and simple solutions to the world's problems. The documentary characterizes Joseph Kony as the personification of evil, shown next to images of Adolph Hitler and Osama bin Laden, figures whom American and European audiences will immediately recognize as one-dimensionally evil leaders (Kurasawa, 2019; Shirley, 2016). The documentary does not delve into the broader conflict that allowed the LRA to commit its crimes, or the accusations of similar crimes against the Ugandan government. The simplicity and succinctness of this narrative gave *Kony 2012* great mobility across social networks (Chazal & Pocrnic, 2016). Though global film festivals may rely on the spectatorship of suffering (Tascón, 2012; see Chapter 4), Kony 2012 represents an innovation in compelling a sense of personal moral responsibility to act in viewers (von Engelhardt & Jansz, 2014). Questions remain, however, about whether sharing with peers and "liking" content on social networking sites, or what some scholars have called "slacktivism," can lead to the sustainable reforms promised by the Kony 2012 campaign (Chazal & Pocrnic, 2016). Too, the Kony 2012 campaign illustrates how media—much like global concerts and film festivals—can become tropish in rendering otherwise very complicated conflicts that have origins and consequences far beyond the boundaries of what a 30-minute documentary could capture, a point that we develop further in Chapter 6.

#BringBackOurGirls

Two years after the Kony 2012 campaign, another global hashtag event created international attention. In mid-April of 2014, 276 female students aged 15–18 were kidnapped from a school in the town of Chibok in northeast Nigeria. Abducted by the Islamic terrorist group Boko Haram, whose name roughly translates in English to "Western education is forbidden" (Njoroge, 2017), the abduction was part of a larger campaign of violence and kidnappings following clashes with the Nigerian government starting in 2010. Up until 2014, Boko Haram had gained territory from the Nigerian government and conducted activities in neighboring Cameroon and Chad. Schools in the area were closed due to the security threats posed by Boko Haram, but the girls were in Chibok to take a physics exam. Following their abduction, the girls, most of whom were Christian, were forced to convert to Islam and marry Boko Haram fighters (Smith & Sherwood, 2014).

This event, which was one attack on a Nigerian school among many by Boko Haram, would have remained a regional concern were it not for the social network campaign "#BringBackOurGirls." In the early days of the campaign, at least one Western journalist lamented the lack of attention the kidnapping was receiving (Ghitis, 2014). As April turned to May, angry parents and other concerned Nigerians rallied in the streets of Lagos and other Nigerian cities dressed in red and white to protest the government's inadequate efforts to release the kidnapped girls. Nigerian lawyer Ibrahim M. Abdullahi authored a tweet with the hashtag #BringBackOurGirls on April 23, 2014; former Federal Minister of Education Obiageli Ezekwesili retweeted Abdullahi's tweet and also used the hashtag in her own tweet later that day (Parkinson & Hinshaw, 2021a). These initial tweets would mobilize the campaign, which aimed to pressure both the Nigerian and American governments to act swiftly to force a safe return of the kidnapped girls (Khoja-Moolji, 2015). Facebook and Twitter accounts were established to track the progress of rescue efforts, which remain active to this day.

By May of 2014, the hashtag had gone viral, reaching a million tweets (Shearlaw, 2015). The rapid spread of the hashtag owed in large part to the participation of prominent American and European celebrities and policymakers. Notable tweeters included Oprah Winfrey, Bill Gates, Chris Brown, Hillary Clinton, and Angelina Jolie. Perhaps most significantly, then-First Lady of the US Michelle Obama tweeted a photo of herself holding a piece of white paper with the hashtag written on it and a brief message in the content of the tweet (Obama, 2014). The tactic of posting a photograph of oneself holding paper with the hashtag written on it was imitated by Pakistani education activist Malala Yousafzai, American comedian Ellen DeGeneres, and others (Clarke, 2019). The official Facebook page for the Bring Back Our Girls campaign organized a Social Media March on May 8, 2014, where users were encouraged to spend 200 minutes "creating awareness" about the kidnapping across their social networking sites (Bring Back Our Girls, 2014).

FIGURE 5.1 First Lady Michelle Obama Holds a Sign with the Hashtag "#BringBackOurGirls"

Reprinted from the @FLOTUS44 Twitter Archives. Posted May 7, 2014.

The campaign eventually took on broader goals than the release of the kidnapped girls, though for the Nigerian activists with whom the campaign originated, this has remained their main objective. For others, primarily those tweeting in the Global North, the hashtag came to also symbolize a critique of Western media outlets that remained largely silent about the horrors committed by Boko Haram (Njoroge, 2017). It also took on meaning as a call to protect the rights of women to have free access to education, as one of Boko Haram's foundational aims is closing schools for girls (Chiluwa & Ifukor, 2015). Since the initial abduction, more than half of the girls are still missing, while about 100 have been released or have escaped (Mbah, 2019). While international attention brought to Boko Haram has led the group to focus its attacks more intently on Nigerian women, commentators have noted that without the hashtag going viral seven nations would not have committed billions of dollars to the search for the kidnapped girls (Parkinson & Hinshaw, 2021b). That over 100 girls remain missing is not a failure of social network activism, but a failure of military efforts.

It is tempting to apply similar critiques to the Bring Back Our Girls campaign as those leveled against the Kony 2012 campaign, as both global hashtag events focused on generating popular interest in an otherwise disinterested Global North about kidnappings in Africa. In both events, the audience in the Global North moved on relatively quickly, while Kony still remains at large and many of the girls are still held hostage. Like Kony 2012, the Bring Back Our Girls campaign may have gained traction so quickly because it fits within a broader, historic narrative of victimhood for Africans in need of saving by Westerners (Maxfield, 2016). However, scholars have warned the comparison often obscures what made the Bring Back Our Girls campaign a unique event (Clarke, 2019; Maxfield, 2016). The original hashtag began in Nigeria, with a grassroots blend of on-the-ground and social network activism (Maxfield, 2016; Njoroge, 2017). The homegrown campaign was taken up by a larger international effort in the Global North and did not quickly dissolve in Nigeria (though it has faded from international attention) (Njoroge, 2017).

In addition, visceral images of the victims were only prevalent in the local campaign. Unlike Kony 2012, such images were not a central element of the international campaign. Rather, Twitter and Facebook users shared a stylized logo that read "#BRING BACK OUR GIRLS" in white block letters on a red background, the colors chosen by the official Facebook page (Clarke, 2019). Finally, as we noted earlier, Invisible Children's proposed solution was catching an individual, whose capture would presumptively end the war. Rather, Bring Back Our Girls aimed more broadly at continuous gender crimes. The use of the possessive "our" creates a global cause; the use of text rather than images of individuals leads to more relatability and a way to connect to the larger social structure for easier distribution (Clarke, 2019). Scholars continue to debate about the extent to which slacktivism, or "do good" activism, represents global civic action in the case of Bring Back Our Girls (see Chiluwa & Ifukor, 2015; Clarke, 2019; Maxfield, 2016; Ofori-Parku & Moscato, 2018). The grassroots organizing of Nigerian activists through social networks is cause for some optimism. Certainly, building awareness and sharing ideas, even if through social networks, is an element of engaged citizenship. The Bring Back Our Girls campaign demonstrates that online and offline activities are not distinct but rather symbiotic (Olson, 2016). That the proposed instrument of justice was relatively simplistic—in both social network events, swift military intervention—calls into question the potentials for global hashtag events to produce broad structural change, or to solve the cycles of violence sustained by the neocolonial global order (Njoroge, 2017).

At-Home Events

To examine another iteration of a digital age global event, we return to Global Citizen, the NGO that produced two concerts broadcast over television and streamed over the internet in April and June of 2020. These at-home events, held in response to the cancellation of in-person concerts due to the COVID-19 pandemic, combined elements of face-to-face global concerts, the previously described global hashtag events, and traditional telethons. Telethons, derived from the words "television" and "marathon," are televised fundraising events that can last hours or days, are aimed at a specific cause or charity, and include celebrity appearances and entertainment. The typical goal of telethons is soliciting financial pledges from the viewing audience. The earliest telethon was hosted by comedian Milton Berle in 1949 for the Damon Runyon Cancer Research Foundation. Since that time, telethons became a tried-and-true vehicle for charities and NGOs looking to raise funds and increase awareness, with some recurring events (such as comedian Jerry Lewis's annual telethon in support of the Muscular Dystrophy Association) but most in response to individual events (such as the Hope for Haiti Now telethon in response to the catastrophic earthquake in 2010). Success in generating donations during telethons is generally owed to three factors: celebrity participation and entertainment, the elicitation of empathy, and the creation of national peer groups (Einolf et al., 2012)

Once a cultural phenomenon, the rise of the internet appears to have reduced the number of NGOs using telethons to generate support and funds. Still, both Global Citizen at-home events in 2020 at least resembled telethons, with multiple-hour broadcasts of prerecorded and live performances and celebrity hosts, both with the aim of spreading awareness about global issues. What distinguishes these events from telethons is the absence of fundraising and their emphasis on engagement over social network platforms. Hugh Evans specifically contrasted the Global Citizen at-home events with traditional telethons, noting that these events eschewed individual fundraising since during the pandemic "people have lost jobs, and that's not the right thing to do right now" (Willman, 2020, para. 8). That Evans felt compelled to contrast these concerts with traditional telethons demonstrates the extent to which they borrowed from the format. While Global Citizen runs an in-person festival each year, these adaptations of their typical offerings are more akin to single-issue events, given that the format and content were both planned in response to the COVID-19 pandemic (Rojek, 2013). As a result, the educational elements of each event were also responsive to the phase of the pandemic in which they were broadcast. In the following subsection, we describe each event individually. We then conclude this chapter by analyzing them together and assessing the extent to which this fusion of live performance, education, and social network interactions represents a new phase of global events.

One World: Together at Home

The first at-home global event, One World: Together at Home, was held on April 18, 2020. An online pre-show was streamed over the course of six hours on YouTube followed by a two-hour special on all three major US broadcast networks (ABC, CBS, and NBC), various cable networks, and a number of digital platforms. Broadly, this event celebrated healthcare workers in the early days of the pandemic and educated viewers about safety measures they could take to prevent the spread of COVID-19. Evans described three goals for Together at Home:

> Firstly, how do you actually end Covid? Which is all about social distancing, testing, and therapeutics and a vaccine. The second thing we're going to focus on: What can you as an individual do locally and globally? We'll still be encouraging people to take action, just not through their money. [...] That's in our DNA. And then the third thing is we want to use this as an opportunity to really encourage governments to invest more in health systems, so that this doesn't happen again. That's all going to be highlighted through the special.
>
> *(Willman, 2020, para. 11)*

Throughout the broadcast, presenters spoke on the need for the general public to help end the COVID-19 pandemic by spending time at home. The performances were framed as a reward to those willing to stay at home. Though not a fund-raising event, the hosts and presenters did take time to highlight donations from Global Citizen's philanthropic and private sector partners, which went to fund the World Health Organization's (WHO) COVID-19 Solidarity Response Fund.

As an eight-hour event, each of the first six hours was hosted by a different celebrity (Jameela Jamil, Matthew McConaughey, Danai Curira, Becky G, Laverne Cox, and Don Cheadle, respectively), with Lady Gaga curating the event and serving as M.C. for the final, most high-profile two hours of the program. Global Citizen did not devote funds to professionally record the performances. The performances themselves were prerecorded, and the production value varied across performers. Most performers played one song in their home studios, backyards, living rooms, etc. Most songs were stripped-down versions of performers' famous songs (either played over acoustic guitars or with minimal accompaniment). As a result, most of the songs were soft, somber, and introspective, with a handful of more pop-oriented songs sprinkled in. The program followed a general format: music performance, brief documentary, and a testimonial/speech from a celebrity/athlete, WHO/UN leader, or medical expert offering advice and support. In this manner, the event itself was relatively repetitive, though we do not believe the planners intended for views to necessarily sit through all six hours. Rather, one could tune in and out of this event and not miss a beat.

Global Goal: Unite for Our Future

Occurring three months after Together at Home, Global Citizen produced their second at-home concert, this time in partnership with the European Commission. On June 27, 2020, Global Goal: Unite for Our Future was broadcast following a fundraising campaign and a summit by the same name. The campaign aimed to respond to the inequitable responses to the COVID-19 pandemic by securing financial commitments from world leaders, corporate partners, and philanthropists. The summit featured journalist-moderated panel discussions with celebrities, political leaders, activists, and medical experts. The concert was a culminating event for the campaign, a celebration of the funds raised in the previous months. Evans stated it was inspired by the "centuries-old concept of music as a motivator for change and unity" (Ramos, 2020, para. 3). As such, the goals of the televised concert were not just congratulatory. Evans remarked that the aims of Unite for Our Future were broader than the ongoing pandemic. Rather, the performances sought to inform a global audience about "how to fight COVID-19, how to fight racial injustice, how to fight sexual injustice" (Amorosi, 2020, para. 4). Thus, Global Citizen aimed to educate as broad an audience as possible with an effort to mitigate the spread of COVID-19 and to build equitable responses to the global pandemic.

As a two-hour event, Unite for Our Future was in some ways a more modest affair than its predecessor with just one host (actor Dwayne Johnson), performers, and celebrity appearances. During the previous at-home concert, the performances were recorded largely in the musicians' homes. Many of the performances during Unite for Our Future were recorded in public places, such as Jennifer Hudson's performance on a boat in the Chicago River or Miley Cyrus's performance in an empty Rose Bowl Stadium. With multiple camera angles, professional editing, dramatic lighting, and flashy visual effects, these performances were more akin to stylized music videos than what one would see at a typical in-person concert. Evans contrasted the spectacle of these performances with other at-home events, saying the goal was to "give the audience an opportunity to dream differently than what they are used to in this moment" (Amorosi, 2020, para. 5). Many of these performances appeared on Global Citizen's YouTube page before the event was broadcast on NBC and MSNBC and streamed on YouTube, Facebook, and other streaming services. Like the first at-home event, Unite for Our Future also featured a familiar format that alternated between performance, documentary, and commentary from a leader, celebrity, or expert.

In the following sections, we explore some of the themes we observed in these at-home events. Overall, there was an emphasis on speaking directly to an audience that in some ways feels more direct than the in-person events we analyzed in Chapter 3. These events also offered audiences more information than did the in-person concerts, not unlike what we observed at the film festivals in Chapter 4. There was less entertainment during at-home events than at in-person concerts, though entertainment remains an important draw for viewers.

Global Civic Goals

COVID-19 and You

The central message of Together at Home, and to a lesser extent Unite for Our Future, is what ordinary people can do to fight the global pandemic. During Together at Home, Irish musician Hozier advised the audience to

> listen to the advice of the World Health Organization and give them all the support that you can. This pandemic respects no borders, or walls, or political persuasions, so it's something that we all have a responsibility to tackle together.

Likewise, American comedian Jack Black performed a series of humorous skits to advise viewers on how they can combat the spread of COVID-19. Many of the between-performance documentaries during Together at Home encouraged viewers to show gratitude toward healthcare workers for their sacrifices made during the pandemic. There was a particular effort to distance the efforts of these shows from fundraising. As actress Jameela Jamil introduced the first hour of Together at Home, she asked the audience for text messages of support but noted that the event was "not a fundraiser, just here to give an incredible show." Co-hosts Jimmy Kimmel, Stephen Colbert, and Jimmy Fallon closed the event with the same basic message as Jamil's opening: Global Citizen has already raised money, but viewers can send text messages to see what they can do to help stop the spread of COVID-19.

Unite for Our Future provided a more focused message than its predecessor. Nearly every speaker linked the efforts to fight COVID-19 with the fight against systemic racism. While fighting racial inequality has always been a goal of Global Citizen, the through line of systemic racism was delivered in more stark terms than in previous Global Citizen events. This event was broadcast one month after the murder of George Floyd by Minneapolis police officers in May of 2020 and the global protest movement that followed. Host Dwayne Johnson invoked Floyd's murder during his opening remarks. Johnson, projecting a serious and mournful tone, linked COVID-19 with another ongoing disease: "oppression and inequality." He went on to describe Floyd's murder as a flashpoint in centuries of race-based oppression and noted that in times of economic and public health crises, the most vulnerable suffer: "Our Black Americans and people of color all around the world have been hit the hardest during these unprecedented times."

As such, a grim, more urgent—yet at times hopeful—air pervaded Unite for Our Future than Together at Home, which was more celebratory and fun, with moments of subdued reflection on the toll of the pandemic. Through it all, there was an effort to speak in a direct manner to the viewing audience. For example, American actress Kerry Washington spoke about structural racism and the extent to which these issues are personal for her. She referenced her familial history— "Black people, my people"—while footage of Black Lives Matter protests ran across the screen. She pressed the viewers to take action:

> As a global community we must now work together to build a better world for all children, everywhere. We are living through a major moment in history. When our children ask what we did to have an impact, I want to be able to tell them that I was a part of the fight for liberation, freedom, and equality for all people. That I answered the call. That is what I will say to my kids. What will you tell yours? I pray that we will continue to build the kind of world that they deserve to live in.

Other efforts to highlight the inequities of the global society came from South African American actress Charlize Theron, whose vignette highlighted the surge in COVID-19 cases across Africa. She noted the pandemic's impact on vulnerable girls and women, imploring leaders to take action in light of the threats to "years of hard-won development progress across the continent [Africa]." Even the Procter & Gamble commercials which ran during the televised broadcast stayed on-theme with the event, blending consumerism and racial justice.

Global to Local

In speaking to an at-home audience—as opposed to in-person concert attendees—both events sought to leverage the intensity of the pandemic to compel action. While the in-person concerts induced action through the Global Citizen app *before* the event (see Chapter 3), these events aimed to educate and inspire everyday actions to combat a unique and ongoing global crisis. Much of the rhetoric between performances noted that COVID-19 is impacting all of humanity and that everyone must find ways to be responsible during a difficult time. In this way, both at-home events used strategies reminiscent of traditional telethons. Viewers of telethons are more likely to give to causes that are domestic rather than international (Bekkers & Wiepking, 2011) and to groups they identify with in some way (Schervish & Havens, 2002). Together at Home featured a compilation of videos from social network posts around the globe where people interacted in socially distanced ways. For instance, one video depicts a woman showing an elderly relative her engagement ring while standing outside a window. Leaders and celebrities offered rhetoric about unity in the face of this global tragedy. Tijjani Muhammad-Bande, President of the UN General Assembly, said, "We are playing our part as global citizens by staying together at home." Similarly, UN Secretary-General H.E. António Guterres referenced the "universal language of music," and said, "together we will defeat this virus and rebuild a fairer world as united global citizens and united nations."

The notion of thinking globally and acting locally was repeated throughout these events. While true of both at-home events, a particular emphasis of

Together at Home was human interest stories about healthcare workers and the sacrifices they have made during the pandemic. Performers also frequently offered gratitude to frontline workers. American actor Matthew Bomer implored viewers to remember the

> importance of taking a global and a local approach to fighting COVID-19. Thinking globally means supporting the World Health Organization to curb the pandemic and prevent future outbreaks. And acting locally means supporting your local charities and initiatives so frontline healthcare workers and those that are at immediate risk have the resources they need to survive.

Performers used cosmopolitan language in making their pleas to viewers to do whatever they can to slow the spread of the COVID-19 pandemic. Puerto Rican musician Luis Fonsi urged viewers to recognize their common humanity: "It doesn't matter where we are from, it doesn't matter what language we speak, what the color of our skin is. It's about being together, being one." British actress Olivia Colman spoke about the mental health challenges brought about by the pandemic, asking the audience for little acts of kindness. This rhetoric of unity during Together at Home often discursively obscured the ways that some people were disproportionately impacted by COVID-19. There were occasional moments where performers such as Beyonce Knowles and Alicia Keys noted that Black Americans are disproportionately affected by COVID-19, with Knowles referencing her hometown of Houston. Otherwise, viewers—save for healthcare workers—were largely positioned as equally impacted by COVID-19 during the Together at Home event.

Though sharper in identifying the inequitable impact of COVID-19, presenters at Unite for Our Future also made a broadly cosmopolitan argument that viewers must act as one. While Johnson bluntly assessed the disproportionate impact of COVID-19 on Black Americans, later he struck a hopeful chord arguing:

> An extraordinary silver lining has emerged: world unity. Unity born in the face of a global health pandemic. Unity born in the face of racial injustice. The events of 2020 have shed a light on a path moving forward, exposing the incredible compassion and empathy that we are capable of achieving when we stand united, active in the mission to normalize equality.

Johnson went on to encourage each "citizen of the world" to participate in the process of improving education, health systems, and sustainability: "Each of us are change agents with a responsibility to bring people together and to make a difference." Johnson is suggesting he, the audience, the corporate sponsors, and the governments who have signed on, are all global citizens working together on a common cause. Similarly, Mexican American actress Salma Hayek described efforts to beat viruses in the past, including her work in Sierra Leone vaccinating people for tetanus. She made a direct plea for action around global citizenship: COVID-19 reminds the viewers that "the entire world population shares problems that do not see boundaries [...] every one of us have to go beyond geographic, economic, and racial boundaries so we can come together and unite as one."

Scientific Learning about COVID-19

Unite for Our Future also had a secondary goal of informing viewers about scientific research into COVID-19. Airing in June of 2020, the possibility of a vaccine to fight the spread of COVID-19 was more of a reality than during Together at Home. As such, many of the documentary featurettes that ran during Unite for Our Future educated viewers about the development and production of the vaccine and who would likely gain access to the vaccine upon its development. The YouTube live broadcast included definitions of terms related to COVID-19 (such as "contact tracing" and "incubation period") where commercial breaks would appear during the televised broadcast. Past outbreaks were used to offer lessons about how scientific research would be used to fight COVID-19. For instance, one short documentary focused on the effort to develop and distribute the vaccine for polio. It featured Bill Gates, a polio survivor, and public health experts who connected the long fight to contain polio to the ongoing efforts around COVID. By highlighting the work of the Global Polio Eradication Initiative, the central message of this documentary was the need for a global deployment of an eventual COVID-19 vaccine. Another brief documentary predicted the likely gaps in healthcare systems' global responses to COVID through the lens of the 2014 Ebola outbreak in West Africa. The narrator noted that "viruses don't respect borders" and examined the systemic boundaries to gaining access to preventative medicine.

In one featurette, Unite for Our Future also responded to the spread of misinformation about COVID-19. Ken Jeong, comedian and licensed physician, dispelled myths about COVID-19 in humorous ways, urging viewers, "Don't deny the science." Other celebrities and performers, such as singer Miley Cyrus and footballer David Beckham, urged viewers to use social networks to pressure leaders to fund research efforts to fight and prevent COVID-19, in a manner similar to the Global Citizen concerts. In another featurette, Danish actor Nikolaj Coster-Waldau tied greenhouse gasses and climate change to the COVID-19 pandemic. He referred to social distancing and lockdowns in the early months of the pandemic, saying, "We all stood up, and we took each other's hands and we did it." He then noted the side effect of the COVID lockdowns was the cleansing of the environment and noted that collective action can have positive or negative effects on the natural world almost instantly. While the pandemic is horrific, Waldau argued that it will pass, but climate change will remain an issue. He concluded by imploring viewers to demand that their leaders take action toward the environment. This was a rare, concentrated call for action toward climate change during either at-home event, which is typically a pillar of Global Citizen's efforts.

Ordinary Heroes

During both at-home events, efforts were made to highlight the work of every-day people to fight the global pandemic. During Together at Home, musical performances were often punctuated by human interest stories narrated by celebrities. Healthcare workers and scientists described not only the long hours spent fighting the pandemic and the risks to their own health, but also the toll this work has taken on their families. Other segments focused on the challenges faced by teachers, who abruptly transitioned to distanced-based learning with the onset of the pandemic, or those working to feed the homeless during the lockdown. Unite for Our Future featured similar stories, though in keeping consistent with its emphasis on the intersection of systemic racism and the pandemic, many focused on equity. For instance, one featurette profiled Dr. Ala Stanford, a pediatric surgeon in Philadelphia whose work transitioned from performing operations to testing for COVID-19 in the Black community. She discussed her motivations for taking on this mandate, noting that her ultimate goal is broader than responding to the current crisis. Rather, she wants to be a part of a movement to change "these health outcomes that disproportionately affect the Black community." Viewers were periodically prompted to show support for those working on the frontlines of the pandemic by texting the word "action" or visiting the Global Citizen website.

Leaders Must Act

While compelling human interest stories were a common feature of both at-home events, there was still a common call for leaders to act in the face of cascading crises. There was consistent talk about how global systemic changes are fostered across both these events and during the in-person concerts analyzed in Chapter 3. During Together at Home, Paul McCartney asked viewers to "tell our leaders they need to strengthen the healthcare systems all around the world so that a crisis like this never happens again." During Unite for Our Future, leaders in government and business spoke about their philanthropic commitments to building a better world for everyone. The Prime Ministers of Spain and Italy argued collaboration was the only path toward defeating COVID-19. Ursula von der Leyen, the president of the European Union, and other public leaders described their nations' and organizations' efforts in fighting COVID-19. P&G, Verizon, and other corporate sponsors plugged their own efforts in a collage of statements (including a statement by FIFA, the International Federation of Association Football, who had a vested interest in getting people back into stadiums and has a dubious track record with slave labor). In another featurette, Canadian Prime Minister Justin Trudeau described how Canada was "doing its part." Other leaders, philanthropists, and representatives from pharmaceutical companies described their nations' and organizations' efforts to solve the COVID crisis. In concluding this sequence, a title card thanked the generosity of the American people— not its government—for the money raised and pledged to "help low-income countries contain and prevent the spread of COVID-19."

Engagement

Few researchers have tried to measure audience engagement during at-home concerts. The few studies that currently exist suggest, unsurprisingly, that audiences exhibit greater engagement with music when attending in-person live events over viewing pre-recorded performances (e.g., Bradby, 2017; Lamont, 2011; Swarbrick et al., 2019). This research was conducted before the COVID-19 pandemic, meaning participants were viewing performances at home at a time when in-person concerts were also an option. With the onslaught of the pandemic and the associated lockdowns, many musicians and organizations made pivots to at-home performances, much like the two Global Citizen events examined in this chapter. One team of researchers sought to better understand the extent to which these livestreamed and prerecorded concerts facilitated the sense of connectivity between audience members and performers, like one would likely feel at an in-person event (Swarbrick et al., 2021). Participants completed a questionnaire asking them about the impact of COVID-19 on their sense of loneliness, isolation, and anxiety. The questionnaire also asked participants about their social engagement during the COVID-19 concerts as gauged by their comments and "likes" in the interactive features of the streaming platforms through which they viewed the performances, as well as participants' reported social network posts about the concerts. This study also measured a concept called *kama muta*—'moved by love' in Sanskrit—which describes the "the warm, positive emotion that we often label as *being moved* as a social relational emotion" (Swarbrick et al., 2021, para. 13).

It is unclear if any of the participants in this study viewed either of the Global Citizen at-home concerts, but the self-reported data illuminates some of our observations. Swarbrick et al. (2021) found evidence of greater social engagement during concerts where the performers explicitly referenced the COVID-19 pandemic during the concerts. They also argued that concerts streamed or televised live, such as the in-person Global Citizen events described in Chapter 3, produced more audience connection than prerecorded concerts, such as the two Global Citizen at-home events. Concurrently, we were able to observe only limited audience interaction during these events, potentially because the performances were prerecorded. For instance, when watching on YouTube Live, viewers could comment in the website's chat function. Many identified from where they were watching, writing "INDONESIA HERE," "Hi, from Malaysia," and "hello from NY," while others would send messages of support to their favorite performers as they performed. The chat moved quickly, speaking perhaps to the volume of people using the platform to interact during performances.

But this also meant viewers did not generally exchange ideas, they only sought to be seen/heard. We observed similar types of interactions on the livestream of the Together at Home event on Facebook, with viewers sending greetings to the performers (much like one would cheer when a performer took the stage), posting supportive emojis and gifs, and occasional comments mocking the performances or the causes being championed by the event.

Global Citizen aimed to inspire social network interaction by promoting the use of #TogetherAtHome and #GlobalGoalUnite in tweeting about these events. A search of the hashtag on Twitter in the days leading up to each event shows the hosts, performers, corporate sponsors (including Cisco, Coca-Cola, Johnson & Johnson, and State Farm), and Global Citizen using the hashtag, but little in the way of ordinary users engaging with it. Perhaps most salient for Global Citizen, Swarbrick et al. (2021) also observed a connection between viewers' empathic concern, or "the social emotions of sympathy and compassion for those experiencing negative events" (para. 65), with their feelings of *kama muta* (or being moved) and connectedness with others while viewing the at-home concerts. If the attendees of Global Citizen's in-person concerts are any indication, those viewing the at-home concerts were likely already sympathetic to the performances and attendant programming.

Impact

Global Citizen boasted that Together at Home was a record-breaking event. In terms of audience reached, it certainly ranks among the most watched global events, airing in over 175 countries and receiving 250 million views either on YouTube, Facebook, or across 60 broadcast networks[1] (Global Citizen, 2020). While education and entertainment were two goals of these at-home events, Global Citizen primarily measured success through the funds raised by each event. Together at Home raised $127.9 million, which went to efforts to mitigate the spread of COVID-19. Indeed, Guinness World Records recognized Together at Home as setting world records for most musical acts to perform at a remote music festival and most money raised for charity by a remote music festival. Craig Glenday, Editor-in-Chief at Guinness World Records, said that Together at Home demonstrated "vividly how the power of music can unite us all and help us through challenging times" (Stephenson, 2020). Global Citizen committed $55.1 million to the WHO's COVID-19 Solidarity Response Fund, while $72.8 million went to local response efforts. In its impact report, Global Citizen highlighted the purchase of PPE, respirators, and test kits, as well as the efforts of corporate sponsors to support international NGOs working in the areas of education, food security, healthcare, and housing (Global Citizen, 2020). As the culmination of months-long fundraising efforts, the results of Unite for Our Future were even more staggering: a total of $6.9 billion was raised, with $1.5 billion committed to grants and $5.4 billion in loans (Global Citizen, 2021). These funds largely came from governments and corporate sponsors. Over $1 billion of these funds was devoted to testing, treatment, and vaccine development. Global Citizen's impact report for the Unite for Our Future campaign emphasized their efforts to disperse funds to agencies serving those made most vulnerable by COVID-19.

Conclusions

In the post-Westphalian order, globalization and social networks have challenged the supremacy of the nation-state as an organizing structure of global order. This novel and unstable realignment challenges the efficacy of institutions of justice tied to national power structures (Fraser, 2009). The issues at play during the events profiled in this chapter, both at-home and hashtag events, speak to transnational social movements yearning for justice while working through the messiness of engaging new tools and modalities of engagement. These events provide examples of how individuals and organizations have used the disaggregated mediaspace as a global forum in appeals for justice. This is nascent event-education in a digitally networked global age, where audiences are no longer considered passive recipients of content, but rather use social networks to cross the "hallowed production/consumption boundary to speak back, remix, navigate and share in familiar and new ways" (Livingstone, 2015, p. 138). The events we reviewed in this chapter were birthed out of the disaggregated nature of information consumption evidenced by the younger generation. It is not simply a matter of skepticism toward traditional news and governmental sources of information. Rather, the younger generation—at least where WIFI and affordable mobile devices are available—is increasingly self-selecting, curating, and sharing content that appeals to their global civic ideologies (Bennett, 2015). Hashtags like #Kony2012 or #BringBackOurGirls are amplified only by user engagement and are thus performative and pedagogical moments of global learning, even if their impact is momentary and fleeting.

The at-home concerts seek to leverage social network user engagement in similar ways while relying on the spectacle of musical performance. Posting about music on social networks—or musicking—helps articulate social, cultural, and subcultural identities toward an imagined audience (Campos, 2019). During both at-home concerts, viewers "shouted out" particular performers in the chat function of YouTube. We presume viewers know Chris Martin of Coldplay is not likely watching the chat during the livestream. Rather, this is an effort to publicly align oneself with the subculture of Coldplay fans. Similar displays of identification with the Global Citizen subculture, or at least the causes championed by this NGO, were events during the at-home events.[2] Though the success of the at-home events was primarily measured through fundraising, the goal appeared to be the mobilization of the masses toward worthy causes through social networks. At the same time, there were inherent restraints to these events not being in-person. The need to document and share one's experience, as opposed to their allegiance, a feature of the global concerts we examined in Chapter 3, was simply not present here. Viewers checked in on YouTube, but would one take a selfie watching from home and post it on Instagram? It's unlikely. At-home events will continue, as Global Citizen was able to raise more funds through their at-home events than their in-person counterparts. However, interest in these events may wane even as our global society becomes increasingly connected by social networks if organizers do not find ways to make these events more experiential.

Lacking the built-in engagement inherent in live performances (Baym, 2018; Lamont, 2011; Pehkonen, 2017; Swarbrick et al., 2019), at-home events rely on the pedagogical strategy of celebrity humanitarianism perhaps more than any other type of event in this book. Borrowing skills from their work as actors, musicians, entrepreneurs, and so on, celebrities engage in a form of performance when using their platforms as public figures to attend to global causes (Street, 2002; Street et al., 2008; Wheeler, 2011) and take up a variety of tropes to present global issues to audiences (Richey & Brockington, 2020). Celebrity endorsements are important to social media cases as they are able to leverage and connect enlarged networks of followers and viewers to generate awareness and engagement. Celebrity participation is a key element of in-person concerts too, but is perhaps more on display in at-home events, particularly as the range of who constitutes a celebrity broadens as the venue/screen shrinks. While it is tempting to view celebrity engagement with at-home global events as individuals using their resources and influence to support good causes, scholars have argued such efforts reify, rather than alleviate, the inequalities of North/South relations (e.g., Belloni, 2007; Budabin, 2020; Budabin & Pruce, 2018; Chouliaraki, 2012; Richey & Brockington, 2020; Weiss, 2016).

At-home events—especially the hashtag events—risk perpetuating and amplifying assumed hierarchies between the Global North and South the extent to which these events frame solutions to global problems as saving a needy other (Richey & Brockington, 2020). Both types of at-home events put the suffering of global others on display in order to inspire an emotional response, a hallmark of the telethons that preceded these at-home events (Batson, 2011; Longmore, 2016). In so doing, at-home events have the potential to produce "an illusion of participation while reinforcing elite practices" (Budabin & Pruce, 2018, p. 745). It seems these at-home events allow for participants to resolve the discomfort between the coziness of their Western lives and the far-away tragedies that the social network posts aim to resolve. Global telecommunications allow us to be aware of seemingly far-away injustices. It is harder to avoid images of distended bellies of famine victims, those whose homes and livelihoods have been lost to climate change, and children kidnapped by terrorist groups. Thus these at-home events are a way to take some form of action in response to global problems, though leveraging the requirement-becomes-conveniences of doing so through mass distribution, via television.

Notes

1 We were unable to locate audience numbers for Unite for Our Future.
2 It should be noted, there were also users who posted negative responses in the chat about the causes pursued by Global Citizen. This is a common phenomenon on social media referred to as "trolling."

References

Amorosi, A. D. (2020, June 29). Global Citizen's Hugh Evans on Jennifer Hudson's river cruise, a fundraising flood of $6.9 billion, and other large and small 'goals.' *Variety.* https://variety.com/2020/music/news/global-citizen-hugh-evans-concert-summit-jennifer-hudson-1234693947/

Bal, A. S., Archer-Brown, C., Robson, K., & Hall, D. E. (2013). Do good, goes bad, gets ugly: Kony 2012. *Journal of Public Affairs, 13*(2), 202–208. doi:10.1002/pa.1475

Batson, C. D. (2011). *Altruism in humans.* Oxford University Press.

Baym, N. K. (2018). *Playing to the crowd: Musicians, audiences, and the intimate work of connection.* NYU Press.

Bekkers, R., & Wiepking, P. (2011). A literature review of empirical studies of philanthropy: Eight mechanisms that drive charitable giving. *Nonprofit and Voluntary Sector Quarterly, 40*(5), 924–973. doi:10.1177/0899764010380927

Belloni, R. (2007). The trouble with humanitarianism. *Review of International Studies, 33*(3), 451–474. doi:10.1017/S0260210507007607

Bennett, W. L. (2003). New media power: The internet and global activism. In N. Couldry & J. Curran (Eds.), *Contesting media power: Alternative media in a networked world* (pp. 17–38). Rowman and Littlefield.

Bennett, W. L. (2015). Changing societies, changing media systems: Challenges for communication theory, research and education. In S. Coleman, G. Moss, & K. Parry (Eds.), *Can the media serve democracy? Essays in honor of Jay G. Blumler* (pp. 151–163). Palgrave Macmillan.

Bonilla, Y., & Rosa, J. (2015). #Ferguson: Digital protest, hashtag ethnography, and the racial politics of social media in the United States. *American Ethnologist, 42*(1), 4–17. doi:10.1111/amet.12112

boyd, d. m., & Ellison, N. B. (2007). Social network sites: Definition, history, and scholarship. *Journal of Computer-Mediated Communication, 13*(1), 210–230. doi:10.1111/j.1083-6101.2007.00393.x

Bradby, B. (2017). Performer-audience interaction in live concerts: Ritual or conversation?. In I. Tsioulakis & E. Hytonen-Ng (Eds.), *Musicians and their audiences: Performance, speech, and mediation* (pp. 86–104). Routledge.

Bring Back Our Girls. (2014, May 8). *Social Media March.* [Event]. Facebook. https://www.facebook.com/events/1448688578709295/

Brough, M. (2012). 'Fair Vanity': The visual culture of humanitarianism in the age of commodity activism. In R. Mukherjee & S. Banet-Wieser (Eds.), *Commodity activism: Cultural resistance in neoliberal times* (pp. 174–194). NYU Press.

Budabin, A. C. (2020). Caffeinated solutions as neoliberal politics: How celebrities create and promote partnerships for peace and development. *Perspectives on Politics, 18*(1), 60–75. doi:10.1017/S153759271900241X

Budabin, A. C., & Pruce, J. R. (2018). The elite politics of media advocacy in human rights. *New Political Science, 40*(4), 744–762. doi:10.1080/07393148.2018.1528062

Campos, R. (2019). *Understanding musicking on social media: Music sharing, sociality and citizenship* [Doctoral dissertation]. https://openresearch.lsbu.ac.uk/item/88x09

Chazal, N., & Pocrnic, A. (2016). Kony 2012: Intervention narratives and the saviour subject. *International Journal for Crime, Justice and Social Democracy, 5*(1), 98–112. doi:10.5204/ijcjsd.v5i1.216

Chiluwa, I., & Ifukor, P. (2015). 'War against our children': Stance and evaluation in *#BringBackOurGirls* campaign discourse on Twitter and Facebook. *Discourse & Society, 26*(3), 267–296. doi:10.1177/0957926514564735

Chouliaraki, L. (2012). The theatricality of humanitarianism: A critique of celebrity advocacy. *Communication and Critical/Cultural Studies, 9*(1), 1–21. doi:10.1080/14791420.2011.637055

Christensen, C. (2011). Discourses of technology and liberation: State aid to net activists in an era of "Twitter revolutions". *The Communication Review, 14*(3), 233–253. doi:10.1080/10714421.2011.597263

Clarke, M. C. (2019). *Affective justice: The International Criminal Court and the Pan-Africanist pushback*. Duke University Press. doi:10.1215/9781478007388

Diamond, L. J. (2010). Liberation technology. *Journal of Democracy, 21*(3), 69–83. doi:10.1353/jod.0.0190

Einolf, C. J., Philbrick, D. M., & Slay, K. (2012). National giving campaigns in the United States: Entertainment, empathy, and national peer group. *Nonprofit and Voluntary Sector Quarterly, 42*(2), 241–261. doi:10.1177/0899764012467230

Esfandiari, G. (2010, June 8). The Twitter devolution. *Foreign Policy, 7.* https://foreignpolicy.com/2010/06/08/the-twitter-devolution/

Fraser, N. (2009). *Scales of justice: Reimagining political space in a globalizing world*. Columbia University Press.

Friedman, T. L. (2006). *The world is flat: A brief history of the twenty-first century*. Farrar, Straus and Giroux.

Gaffney, D. (2010). *#iranelection: Quantifying online activism* [Paper presentation]. WebSci10: Extending the Frontiers of Society, Online Conference.

Gerbaudo, P. (2014). Populism 2.0: Social media activism, the generic internet user and interactive direct democracy. In D. Trottier & C. Fuchs (Eds.), *Social media, politics and the state: Protests, revolutions, riots, crime and policing in the age of Facebook, Twitter and YouTube* (pp. 67–87). Routledge.

Ghitis, F. (2014, May 28). Why no international effort for 200 kidnapped girls? *CNN.* https://www.cnn.com/2014/05/01/opinion/ghitis-nigeria-kidnapped-girls/

Giroux, H. (2009, June 19). The Iranian uprisings and the challenge of the new media. *CounterPunch.* https://www.counterpunch.org/2009/06/19/the-iranian-uprisings-and-the-challenge-of-the-new-media/

Global Citizen. (2020). *One World Together at Home Global Citizen 6 month impact report.* https://drive.google.com/file/d/1hYytmm5Ri0cRqp0OmGGPD-k5IL1GXyVU/view

Global Citizen. (2021, April 15). *Global Goal United for Our Future Global Citizen 6-month impact report.* https://www.globalcitizen.org/en/content/global-goal-unite-6-month-impact-covid-19/

González-Bailón, S., Borge-Holthoefer, J., Rivero, A., & Moreno, Y. (2011). The dynamics of protest recruitment through an online network. *Scientific Reports, 1*(1), 197. doi:10.1038/srep00197

Greenblatt, A. (2012, March 8). Joseph Kony is infamous—But will he be caught? *National Public Radio.* https://www.npr.org/2012/03/08/148239201/joseph-kony-is-now-a-star-but-will-he-be-caught

Harlow, S. (2012). Social media and social movements: Facebook and an online Guatemalan justice movement that moved offline. *New Media & Society, 14*(2), 225–243. doi:10.1177/1461444811410408

Harris, P. (2012, March 17). Kony 2012: Campaigner's meltdown brought on by stress says wife. *The Guardian.* https://www.theguardian.com/world/2012/mar/17/kony-2012-meltdown-stress-wife

Holligan, A. (2012, March 12). Kony 2012: Prosecutor Ocampo still backing campaign. *BBC News.* https://www.bbc.com/news/av/world-africa-17336033

Invisible Children. (2012, March 5). *KONY 2012* [Video]. YouTube. https://www.youtube.com/watch?v=Y4MnpzG

Jenkins, H. (2006). *Convergence culture: Where the old and new media collide.* New York University Press.

Kanczula, A. (2012, April 20). Kony 2012 in numbers. *The Guardian.* https://www.theguardian.com/news/datablog/2012/apr/20/kony-2012-facts-numbers

Karlin, B., & Matthew, R. A. (2012). Kony 2012 and the mediatization of child soldiers. *Peace Review 24*(3), 255–261. doi:10.1080/10402659.2012.704222

Keating, J. (2012, March 7). Guest post: Joseph Kony is not in Uganda (and other complicated things). *Foreign Policy.* https://foreignpolicy.com/2012/03/07/guest-post-joseph-kony-is-not-in-uganda-and-other-complicated-things/

Khoja-Moolji, S. (2015). Becoming an "intimate publics": Exploring the affective intensities of hashtag feminism. *Feminist Media Studies, 15*(2), 347–350. doi:10.1080/14680777.2015.1008747

Kompatsiaris, P., & Mylonas, Y. (2014). The rise of Nazism and the web: Social media as platforms of racist discourses in the context of the Greek economic crisis. In D. Trottier & C. Fuchs (Eds.), *Social media, politics and the state: Protests, revolutions, riots, crime and policing in the age of Facebook, Twitter and YouTube* (pp. 109–130). Routledge.

Kurasawa, F. (2019). On humanitarian virality: Kony 2012, or, the rise and fall of a pictorial artifact in the digital age. *Visual Communication, 18*(3), 399–423. doi:10.1177/1470357219851807

Lamont, A. (2011). University students' strong experiences of music: Pleasure, engagement, and meaning. *Musicae Scientiae, 15*(2), 229–249. doi:10.1177/1029864911403368

Livingstone, S. (2015). Audiences and publics: Reflections on the growing importance of mediated participation. In S. Coleman, G. Moss, & K. Parry (Eds.), *Can the media serve democracy? Essays in honor of Jay G. Blumler* (pp. 132–140). Palgrave Macmillan.

Longmore, P. K. (2016). *Telethons: Spectacle, disability and the business of charity.* Oxford University Press.

Maxfield, M. (2016). History retweeting itself: Imperial feminist appropriations of "Bring Back Our Girls." *Feminist Media Studies, 16*(5), 886–900. doi:10.1080/14680777.2015.1116018

Mbah, F. (2019, April 14). Nigeria's Chibok schoolgirls: Five years on, 112 still missing. *Al Jazeera.* https://www.aljazeera.com/news/2019/4/14/nigerias-chibok-schoolgirls-five-years-on-112-still-missing.

Miller, D., Costa, E., Haynes, N., McDonald, T., Nicolescu, R., Sinanan, J., Spyer, J., Venkatraman, S., & Wang, X. (2016). *How the world changed social media.* UCL Press.

Miller, N. (2012, April 22). Catch Kony campaign loses couch potatoes. *The Age.* https://www.theage.com.au/technology/catch-kony-campaign-loses-couch-potatoes-20120421-1xdqc.html

Mollins, J. (2012, April 5). *Not enough focus on child soldiers' lives in "Kony 2012".* Thomson Reuters Foundation. https://web.archive.org/web/20120705072012/; http://www.

trust.org/alertnet/blogs/technotalk/not-enough-focus-on-child-soldiers-lives-in-kony-2012-war-child

Morozov, E. (2011). *The net delusion: How not to liberate the world.* Penguin.

Njoroge, D. (2017). Global activism on Facebook: A discursive analysis of "Bring Back Our Girls" campaign. In R. Andersen & P. L. de Silva (Eds.), *The Routledge companion to media and humanitarian action* (pp. 450–464). Routledge.

Obama, M. [@FLOTUS44]. (2014, May 7). *Our prayers are with the missing Nigerian girls and their families. It's time to #BringBackOurGirls. -mo* [Tweet]. Twitter. https://twitter.com/FLOTUS44/status/464148654354628608?s=20&t=MuuSGJ9viJdDwaWXhwRUfw

Ofori-Parku, S. S., & Moscato, D. (2018). Hashtag activism as a form of political action: A qualitative analysis of the #BringBackOurGirls campaign in Nigerian, UK, and U.S. Press. *International Journal of Communication, 12,* 2480–2502.

Okwonga, M. (2012, March 7). Stop Kony yes. But don't stop asking questions. *The Independent.* https://web.archive.org/web/20120308224457/; http://blogs.independent.co.uk/2012/03/07/stop-kony-yes-but-dont-stop-asking-questions/

Olson, C. C. (2016). #BringBackOurGirls: Digital communities supporting real-world change and influencing mainstream media agendas. *Feminist Media Studies, 16*(5), 772–787. doi:10.1080/14680777.2016.1154887

Parkinson, J., & Hinshaw, D. (2021a, March 2). How a hashtag went viral—and incited a military intervention. *WIRED.* https://www.wired.com/story/bring-back-our-girls-international-rallying-cry/

Parkinson, J., & Hinshaw, D. (2021b, April 16). How Twitter activism turned the fight against Boko Haram upside down. *The Washington Post.* https://www.washingtonpost.com/outlook/slacktivism-chibok-twitter-our-girls/2021/04/16/0e3b9fee-9e1f-11eb-8005-bffc3a39f6d3_story.html

Pehkonen, S. (2017). Choreographing the performer–audience interaction. *Journal of Contemporary Ethnography, 46*(6), 699–722. doi: 10.1177/0891241616636663

Poell, T. (2014). Social media activism and state censorship. In D. Trottier & C. Fuchs (Eds.), *Social media, politics and the state: Protests, revolutions, riots, crime and policing in the age of Facebook, Twitter and YouTube* (pp. 189–208). Routledge.

Ramos, D. (2020, June 22). Dwayne Johnson to host Global Citizen's 'Global Goal: Unite for Our Future—The Concert'; Jennifer Hudson, Billy Port, Charlize Theron and more to appear. *Deadline.* https://deadline.com/2020/06/dwayne-johnson-global-citizens-global-goal-unite-for-our-future-the-concert-jennifer-hudson-billy-porter-shakira-charlize-theron-covid-19-coronavirus-1202966123/

Richey, L. A., & Brockington, D. (2020). Celebrity humanitarianism: Using tropes of engagement to understand North/South relations. *Perspectives on Politics, 18*(1), 43–59. doi:10.1017/S1537592719002627

Rojek, C. (2013). *Event power: How global events manage and manipulate.* SAGE.

Rozen, L. (2012, March 8). Kony 2012: Invisible Children's viral video sparks criticism that others say is unfounded. *Yahoo News.* https://news.yahoo.com/blogs/envoy/kony2012-invisible-children-viral-video-uganda-conflict-sparks-183106657.html?guccounter=1

Salem, S. (2014). Creating spaces for dissent: The role of social media in the 2011 Egyptian revolution. In D. Trottier & C. Fuchs (Eds.), *Social media, politics and the state: Protests, revolutions, riots, crime and policing in the age of Facebook, Twitter and YouTube* (pp. 171–188). Routledge.

Schervish, P. G., & Havens, J. J. (2002). The Boston Area Diary Study and the moral citizenship of care. *Voluntas, 13*(1), 47–71. doi:10.1023/A:1014758113132

Shearlaw, M. (2015, April 14). Did the #bringbackourgirls campaign make a difference in Nigeria? *The Guardian.* https://www.theguardian.com/world/2015/apr/14/nigeria-bringbackourgirls-campaign-one-year-on

Shirley, A. T. (2016). KONY 2012: Branding the enemy—Activism imagery in the age of social media and the political brand. *Journal of Media and Religion, 15*(1), 43–59. doi: 10.1080/15348423.2015.1131044

Smith, D., & Sherwood, H. (2014, May 14). Military operation launched to locate kidnapped Nigerian girls. *The Guardian.* https://www.theguardian.com/world/2014/may/14/nigeria-launches-military-operation-to-find-kidnapped-girls

Stephenson, K. (2020, May 22). One World: Together at Home makes history by breaking two records as part of pandemic relief efforts. *Guinness World Records.* https://www.guinnessworldrecords.com/news/2020/5/one-world-together-at-home-makes-history-by-breaking-two-records-as-part-of-pand-618986

Street, J. (2002). Bob, Bono and Tony B: The popular artist as politician. *Media, Culture and Society, 24,* 433–441. doi:10.1177/016344370202400309

Street, J., Hague, S., & Savigny, H. (2008). Playing to the crowd: The role of music and musicians in political participation. *British Journal of Politics and International Relations, 10,* 269–285. doi:10.1111/j.1467-856x.2007.00299.x

Swarbrick, D., Bosnyak, D., Livingstone, S. R., Bansal, J., Marsh-Rollo, S., Woolhouse, M. H., & Trainor, L. J. (2019). How live music moves us: Head movement differences in audiences to live versus recorded music. *Frontiers in Psychology, 9,* 1–11. doi:10.3389/fpsyg.2018.02682

Swarbrick, D., Seibt, B., Grinspun, N., & Vuoskoski, J. K. (2021). Corona concerts: The effect of virtual concert characteristics on social connection and *Kama Muta. Frontiers in Psychology, 12,* 1–21. doi:10.3389/fpsyg.2021.648448

Tascón, S. M. (2012). Considering human rights films, representation, and ethics: Whose face? *Human Rights Quarterly, 34*(3), 864–883. doi:10.1353/hrq.2012.0057

Thrall, A. T., Stecula, D., & Sweet, D. (2014). May we have your attention please? Human-rights NGOs and the problem of global communication. *The International Journal of Press/Politics, 19*(2), 135–159. doi:10.1177/1940161213519132

Von Engelhardt, J., & Jansz, J. (2014). Challenging humanitarian communication: An empirical exploration of Kony 2012. *International Communication Gazette, 76*(6), 464–484. doi:10.1177/1748048514533861

Weiss, T. G. (2016). *Humanitarian intervention.* Polity Press.

Wheeler, M. (2011). Celebrity diplomacy: United Nations' Goodwill Ambassadors and messengers of peace. *Celebrity Studies, 2*(1), 6–18. doi:10.1080/19392397.2011.543267

Williams, B. T., & Zenger, A. A. (2012). Introduction: Popular culture and literacy in a networked world. In B. T. Williams & A. A. Zenger (Eds.), *New media literacies and participatory popular culture across borders* (pp. 1–14). Routledge.

Willman, C. (2020, April 16). How Lady Gaga's 'war room' helped Global Citizen's 'Together at Home' special come together in a flash. *Variety.* https://variety.com/2020/music/news/global-citizen-hugh-evans-interview-one-world-together-at-home-lady-gaga-1234582406/

Wojcieszak, M., & Smith, B. (2014). Will politics be tweeted? New media use by Iranian youth in 2011. *New Media & Society, 16*(1), 91–109. doi:10.1177/1461444813479594

Zeb, A., Khattak, M. K., Jamal, H., & Khattak, A. K. (2016). Analysis of digital democracy's promotion through social media. *New Horizons, 10*(1), 95.

6

LEARNINGS FROM GLOBAL EVENTS

We began researching this book in late 2019, having conceptualized it in 2017. At that time, we had a vision for this book inspired by how we understood the relatively brief, but compelling, lineage of global events. Our original abstract for this book began by listing daunting global issues that inspired the work of global events: climate change, refugee crises, war, poverty, and hunger. Conspicuously absent from our list was the spread of highly contagious diseases and inequitable access to preventative medicine. We collected data at several events in the US and Canada in the fall of 2019, blissfully unaware that this research, and global events themselves, would be completely interrupted by a worldwide health crisis and related economic collapse that, as of writing in 2022, remains a predicament with which governments, health experts, and individuals continue to grapple. We intended to collect data throughout 2020 at events in Africa and Asia, but the COVID-19 pandemic made such efforts impossible. Ironically, the pandemic that suspended in-person global events was the type of calamity to which global events were designed to respond. And thus, at-home events were organized by NGOs through social network engagement, inspiring a global event modality not on our radar when we began this research.

Throughout the writing of this book, we analyzed global events through the lens of two global educators. But we could not avoid considering these events also as consumers of music and films. Writing from Philadelphia, it is hard not to be reminded of the ways Live Aid is stitched into the fabric of this city's cultural history. This seminal global event was held in 1985 just months after the city's police department bombed a West Philadelphia rowhome and let several city blocks burn—the now infamous MOVE bombing. The two events— one a joyous, record-breaking charity concert aimed at ending famine in Ethiopia, the other an unjustified attack by a local government on a back-to-nature

DOI: 10.4324/9780429281570-6

organization whose members were primarily African American—occupy starkly different places in the city's history. Live Aid is a triumphant moment, with Philadelphia-based publications and websites periodically offering readers retrospectives on this moment of civic pride (see Fiorillo, 2020; Kiner, 2020). The collective memory here is that Live Aid was a success, irrespective of its material impact on the Ethiopian famine. The stories that get told about Live Aid are about how the concert brought together a city, and the world, in service of a noble cause, despite the police brutality and racial and economic disparities that plagued, and continue to plague, Philadelphia and beyond. Meanwhile, the MOVE bombings have remained a relatively obscure event, with the city only recently beginning to come to terms with this travesty and its legacy (WHYY Staff, 2021). Live Aid was the best humanity could do; the MOVE bombings were among the worst.

And yet, while almost 30 years since Live Aid the event itself is remembered fondly, there is also a certain skepticism about global events as an approach to solving the world's problems. This feeling is perhaps best exemplified by a 2011 episode of the NBC sitcom *30 Rock*. *30 Rock* depicted the behind-the-scenes antics of a fictitious sketch comedy show, based in part on creator, writer, and star Tina Fey's experiences at *Saturday Night Live*. In this episode, titled "Operation Righteous Cowboy Lightning," corporate boss Jack Donaghy, played by Alec Baldwin, seeks to reinvent himself after the parent company of NBC is bought by a new commercial entity. Donaghy believes that the most successful television programs are celebrity-hosted charity events responding to natural disasters. The only problem for Donaghy is that all the networks run these televised events simultaneously, negating whatever ratings windfall one would hope to reap from organizing and broadcasting such an event. Donaghy then plots to pre-tape the next charity event, creating televised celebrity benefit programs for every possible natural disaster, thus putting NBC in a position to run the next global event before their competitors can produce their own television specials. When Fey's character Liz Lemon warns Donaghy that his unabashed greed would lead to bad karma, he exclaims, "The people affected will still get money, but so will NBC. Everybody wins!" A song is recorded, and actor Robert DeNiro records a series of pleas to respond to a variety of natural disasters. Donaghy is ecstatic when, in the second half of the episode, a typhoon is reported to have hit an island in the South Pacific. Donaghy puts his plan into motion and begins airing the pre-taped celebrity event, only to find out the island is owned by controversial actor Mel Gibson. Despite the televised broadcast being a mess and only benefiting a much-maligned celebrity, the event earns enormous ratings and is a boon to Donaghy's career.

Much of the episode is a critical take on celebrity humanitarianism and the event industry in general. In a scene unrelated to the central plot of this episode, Tracy Jordan, one of the stars of the show around which *30 Rock* is based (played by *Saturday Night Live* alum Tracy Morgan), describes an "elite level of actor craziness" that is acceptable for people who have attained a certain level of fame. Among a list of absurd and bad behaviors, Jordan says dismissively, "speaking to the U.N. about some messed up crap in Africa." That a show as sharp as *30 Rock*, a prime-time network comedy recognized for its insightful but cutting humor, brought its satirical lens to global events speaks to their unquestioned place in the cultural lexicon. Since George Harrison and Ravi Shankar organized the Concert for Bangladesh in 1971, the Western public has come to assume that of an array of responses to global calamities, an event fueled by entertainment, education, and charity will occupy a prominent space. But as with many "do good" efforts that have become commonplace, this send-up of global events reveals a pessimistic understanding of why organizations deploy them, and who ultimately benefits.

To what extent does this satirical vision of global events match with the findings in our book? As the previous chapters have made clear, global events have had their detractors. In particular, scholars before us have criticized the role of celebrity activism in global events (Chouliaraki, 2006; Dayan & Katz, 1992; Tester, 2001). This squares with Tina Fey's vision of clueless celebrities lending their voices to support response efforts to not-yet-happened tragedies in *30 Rock*, lampooning their involvement as a self-centered ploy for attention and career opportunities. Consider that only two people gain any material relief from this fictitious charity event: Mel Gibson, himself a reviled celebrity, and NBC executive Jack Donaghy, capitalism personified. Likewise, Tracy Jordan's quip about actors speaking before the UN is likely a reference to the humanitarian efforts of Angelina Jolie, George Clooney, and other Hollywood actors who have used their clout to try and effect change on a global scale, yet lack the training and on-the-ground experience to understand the nuances of complex geopolitical situations. While this episode aired a full year before *Kony 2012* was released, it is easy to see parallels between the well-intentioned slacktivism embedded in Invisible Children's strategies (Chazal & Pocrnic, 2016) and the caricaturing of audience engagement with faraway tragedies in this episode. That the jokes in this episode are so effective speaks to some truth in the comedy of this take on global events.

After spending the better part of two years researching and thinking about global events, we are not as pessimistic about their potentials. But we might not buy the nostalgia that typifies how the Concert of Bangladesh and Live Aid are remembered either. The value of Global Citizen concerts, for example, is illuminated by the consciousness-raising that these high-profile events create. The fact that they are now a regular event occurring with a cadence closely tied to the annual opening of the General Assembly of the UN helps to solidify in the public consciousness an institution with a mission, however ambiguous the latter may be.

But what else? We aim to address this question first by way of a summary of what we found in the three venues of public pedagogy explored herein—concerts, film festivals, and social network events. Following that, we point to three synthetic, thematic strands that constitute the foundation of the work and the potential for the most trenchant insights to emerge. The summaries will be purposely brief and high-level, foregrounding some of the granular insights from the cases so that the syntheses make sense in light of the details offered.

Global Citizen concerts represent a cosmopolitan response to ongoing global inequalities, rather than one-off events responding to crises of the moment. They have taken on a rhythm of regularity as they are now coincident with the opening of the UN in New York City, a strategic choice to co-locate global policy leaders and challenges of global problems in time and space. The Global Citizen app, designed primarily as a portal to the event, works as a pedagogical-behavioral tool, rewarding global civic activities that permit access and implicitly underscore the values and beliefs that accompany what it means to be a global citizen in the context of contemporary discourse, potentially altering lifestyle choices as a prelude to the concert in the hope that these activities become routinized into everyday life, long after the event is completed. Global Citizen concerts are, however, primarily about the grand show or big spectacle moment. The lights, lasers, stage, special effects, context of Central Park, and build-up to the event, all of it is lassoed to the fame of the performers and energized through the aesthetic and emotional back-and-forth between artists and attendees.

The spectacle then becomes a motivating tool to entice a broader audience—one much larger than what a call to "talk about sustainable development" would ever create—while using the space in between performances to educate audience-goers about global issues. Attending the first Mumbai concert in 2016, I turned and asked an attendee what the concert was all about and they replied, "It's something to do with making the world a better place, but I came to see Chris Martin!" which perhaps best sums up how most attendees understand global concerts. Audience members also are largely sympathetic to the refrain of making the world a better place, with some noteworthy exceptions, and are compelled to act to gain access via the app with a hope on the part of organizers that they will habitualize these motivated changes into long-term life adjustments. From the vantage point of producers, global concerts come to symbolize a commitment to doing good in the world coupled with enhancing fundraising for specific needs and championing policy changes by activating a larger network of supporters. Yet, despite the aim for policy-level change, the concerts are largely focused on the immediacy of the given moment—pandemic-related needs and systemic racism, given the temporal situation of the concerts we happened to study.

Global film festivals, in contrast to the concerts, represent much smaller events occurring over longer periods of time (e.g., a week versus an evening) which focus on learning more deeply about global issues in a somewhat episodic manner. The attendees are largely passive in how they are positioned by the public pedagogy, spending most of their time viewing, with smaller episodes of conversation or shopping in the auxiliary event space. The content of the festivals is largely focused on the condition of others—be it endangered species, victims of abuse.

Indigenous people, or historical figures—but often personified and made emblematic through the precision of a single or small set of stories, rendered in the "truth modality" of the documentary. Attendees shared awareness, however, of the positionality afforded them in being the observers and not the observed, and organizers made efforts to suspend this barrier by inviting film participants and/or directors into conversation with festival-goers. This somewhat displaced the othering inherent in viewing films about others, though not entirely, and that recognition was palpable in conversations we had with organizers and attendees alike. That those viewed were typically of or from the global South further illustrated the familiar dynamic of who is talking about global issues, who is the subject and who is the object, in a sense.

Aesthetic responses to the films were clearly on the minds of the organizers and attendees. Producers tried to organize films to add levity and beauty periodically amidst the overwhelmingly harsh and heavy contents embedded in the documentaries. We experienced, and witnessed other attendees experiencing, the fatigue of horror upon horror with only glimmers of hope within the curriculum of the film set. The shock of the films may have been temporary, however, given that none of the attendees either in the experience itself or in reflection afterward indicated a lessening of commitment to engage with global issues and learning about the world. And many commented in hindsight that the auxiliary events and places in between the films were valued as a release valve of the sheer magnitude of negative contents along with an opportunity for affiliative conversations about who we are and why we engage this work through the prism of festival experiences. More careful consideration of how festivals unfold as a curriculum, or course of learning, is needed in order to modulate the magnitude of the existential crises and personal tragedies on display with meaningful episodes of hope, action, and possibility.

Social network events illustrate a new forum of engagement, one that creates a new venue for transnational social movements oriented toward justice and eliminating suffering. Young people generally are increasingly curating, sharing, and amplifying memes, messages, and contents that appeal to others toward activating policy or interventions into situations that call out the need for intervention. Hashtags like #Kony2012 or #BringBackOurGirls are amplified and networked by user engagement and create performative, pedagogical moments of global learning that are compelling in the moment but also fleeting in impact, due in part to the constancy and intensity of the global mediascape. At-home events rely on the pedagogical strategy of celebrity humanitarianism, perhaps more than any other type of event profiled herein, as they use the personage of famous people to engage an online audience in an intimate way, through the medium of the living room or nearby device. At-home events will continue, but may remain on the fringes even as our global society becomes increasingly connected by social networks, if organizers do not find ways to make these events more experiential. The creation of new broadband technologies that allows direct user interface with media (e.g., talking with performers at an event in real-time, thus creating instant audience engagement) may create more opportunities for at-home events to bridge the gap between performers and audience.

Insights into Three Dynamics

The following insights are presented as dynamics—or complex interactions of social phenomena—that resonated across the cases and modalities in this book, ones that return us to the larger issues of media receptivity, public pedagogy, and global citizenship education (GCE) with which we began in Chapter 1.

D1—Reinscription of North/South Dichotomies within the Frame of One, Polyphonous World

The gulf between invocations of a singular planet revolving placidly in the lonely emptiness of space and the lived realities of life for people on Earth only seems to grow as much as we attempt to name, know, and eradicate that gap. Put simply, we are not yet one world despite our presumed desire to become one. Oxfam releases an annual update on the gap, demonstrating in shocking simplicity the wealth gap between North and South, which Oxfam calls "economic violence" due to structural policies that favor the titular wealthiest above all others. Most recently, the report indicated that 99% of the world's population suffered economically due to Covid-19 while the wealth of the 10 richest men doubled in the same time period. Twenty of the richest people on Earth are emitting 8,000 times more carbon dioxide than 1 billion of the poorest people on the planet (Oxfam, 2022). The global events profiled herein are hyper-aware of the enormity of the gap and yet ill-fitted to make meaningful changes to address it. The fact that redistributive wealth policies—both between and among countries—are needed to rectify this imbalance is far off the agenda of these events. The focus within the spectacle on a colorful and diverse world coming together in a global city to share sentiments—expressed in film, meme, and song—about the world being a better place is about as deep as it goes.

There are moments when the facade of "one world" is exposed, pushing back the curtain in the performance to demonstrate the real gap that exists between the world's haves and have-nots. While I attended the Mumbai Global Citizen Concert in 2016, I was surprised to see the attendees grouped, with VIPs directly in front of the stage and others coordinated in roped-off areas farther away, depending on the color of their ticket, with some attendees as much as a half kilometer away. This affluence gap is deeply embedded in the organization of most events, though what makes these divisions striking is when the content of the events is oriented around such goals as eliminating extreme poverty. Too, that these events are typically housed in major, global cities—such as Mumbai, New York, and San Francisco—also creates significant isolation from the people and situations made most central in the content of the events.

The introduction of musical artists unknown to the commercial music scene, and the need for artists such as George Harrison and Chris Martin to coach the audience to listen to and respect the music, are among the most glaring episodes in the work that we examined, though we are sure more exist. Some would rightly argue that knowing music from around the world and the chasmic and growing wealth gap in the world are two very different issues, and on this, we would concur. Though we think these moments illustrate the starkly different worlds that are represented in these "one world" forums such that beyond songs on "Western terms" they can be unrecognizable to each other. This dynamic, we argue, is present in all aspects of life and serves as an obstacle to making significant and fundamental changes in how the world is structured and who benefits from that organization. The deck is so clearly stacked, perhaps never more evident than in the maldistribution of COVID-19 vaccines. The US, for example, has 178 doses of vaccine for every 100 people, a high average given the presence of booster shots in addition to the original doses, while the Democratic Republic of Congo has 4 per 100 people (WHO Coronavirus Dashboard as of July 19, 2022). And this is just one comparison on a pertinent issue in a sea of potential contrasts that all point to the same fact: a chasmic and widening affluence gap between North and South. The idea that concerts, film festivals, and social networking events can solve this calamity is naive to the point of danger. Rather, structural changes in global finance, infrastructure, and opportunities, along the lines of those benchmarks outlined in SDG 9 (infrastructure) and SDG 10 (reduced inequalities), must be taken seriously by global leaders if this situation is going to be addressed.

D2—Cursory Awareness and Surface, Spectacle Learning of Complex Issues in the Plebiscite of an Emerging Global Public

Events like those studied highlight the related problems of simplification, slacktivism, and superficial engagement. This was glaringly evident in the Kony 2012 social network phenomenon as most participants were "liking" posts as a form of slacktivism and possessing very little knowledge of the complexity of the civil conflict in Uganda. Thus, these entertainment/educational events seem destined to value simplifications on the educational side as a way of privileging the entertaining aspects (e.g., celebrations around changing the world). The fact that there has been a rapid increase in the numbers of these events in comparison to the earlier era that we examine in Chapter 2 suggests that they fill a need on the part of organizers and attendees. Though beyond raising awareness about a range of global issues, it is not altogether clear if there is a larger intention at work or one that can be fulfilled through this medium. A wider aim might be the creation of forums for engaging global issues in a deeper, more sustaining manner.

The global public, like any public, needs mechanisms and spaces for people to voice their ideas, concerns, and hopes, a place where people can be heard and indeed policymakers and leaders are listening. The aim of a global commons emerging in the form of social media networks, an idea very much present at the origin of social media over a decade ago, has quickly devolved into a place of misinformation, conspiracy theorizing, and flaming/ridicule. Alternatively, one could imagine global events like those studied becoming a form of gathering where views can be expressed, shared, and challenged, fitting the plebiscite need as well. Yet, a pattern in our data clearly shows that many of the participants had only a cursory awareness of the event in which they were participants, especially the concerts, and only passing interest in extending their awareness beyond the event itself. With respect to the film festivals, there was greater knowledge and engagement among participants, but these events attracted minuscule numbers compared to the mass events we studied. The most that organizers can claim of the events studied is that they generate cursory awareness within the event itself along with some opportunities for extended learning in auxiliary activities (e.g., the Peace Village or Marketplace of the Future) or in the preceding activities (e.g., Global Citizen's use of an app to record points/activities for concert entry).

But the idea that a concert, film festival, or social networking event can become a forum and a portal for deeper learning does seem to have merit. The events are overly focused in our view as too fixated on the event without enough attention to the pedagogical dimensions of the engagement. This was abundantly clear in the film festivals which lacked either a cohesive plan for the events so they could be more fully realized as learning encounters or lacked dedicated learning spaces within the forums. Rather, the focus really was on the films themselves and the learning, as it were, was left to those in attendance. One could imagine any of these events having an explicit learning guide that would assist participants in positioning themselves as learners vis-à-vis the experience and would offer opportunities to extend dialogues, deepen encounters with contents, and sustain more closely guided study. The convenings themselves are actually quite convenient toward these ends as they have a ready audience, already with a cursory awareness, that through the right kinds of extension opportunities could manifest a substantial pedagogical engagement with the contents. The details of these ideas demand more development, to be sure, but that there is a glaring need to attend carefully to the pedagogical aspects of these events is apparent through our study.

D3—A Motif of Sustainable Consumerism Foreclosing Deeper Structural Changes

The idea of the once-popularized phrase "doing well by doing good" perhaps best summarizes the motif of sustainable consumption that we witnessed throughout all of the events. That one could have a concert where funds were raised, awareness was generated about global problems, and some people made money epitomizes this dimension. Or, that women who were victimized by sex traffickers could "turn things around" through selling jewelry, as presented at the MLJFF Peace Village, was another form of this profit-by-peace approach. Sponsorship of concerts, ad space sold within social media networks, and attendance fees and donations all shape in various ways how these events are brought into the economic matrix of Western capitalism. Indeed, the SDG 15–30 framework is itself premised on the "lift all boats" model of economic development, meaning that the lot of all people can improve by growing the whole economic pie, making sure to adjust the distribution of those gains to those in the lowest earning quintile, for example. Whether that economic growth is actually sustainable, however, is rarely raised as a central concern of those engaging the discourse, assuming that the economic model "is what it is" and we are compelled to do good things within its parameters.

Perhaps this situation cannot be otherwise and as pedagogues, not global economists, we are in no position to offer expert opinion on this broad issue. Yet, given the taken-for-granted nature of the events and their foundations, we worry that failing to underscore these choices as choices forecloses opportunities to engage in a big conversation about what changes may be needed. A case in point is the Marketplace of the Future that accompanied the 2019 Global Citizen Concert in New York City. The notion of "doing well by doing good" was very much in evidence throughout as young, social entrepreneurs were engaged in explaining (and selling) their start-ups to the eco-friendly audience who attended the side event (see Figure 6.1). But what is also missing, pedagogically, is any consideration of alternatives. One of the vendors, for example, shared information about their company which is working on carbon sequestration in concrete. The idea is very attractive as it is a form of green building that allows the current order of build–profit–destruct–and rebuild to continue, seemingly forever, while attending to the need to reduce carbon emissions from concrete-making and to sequester carbon. But the idea that the cycle of build/rebuild itself is not sustainable is hidden or removed from the conversation, as well as the deeper logic of how value is assigned in Western capitalism.

Western capitalism generally views the biosphere as a limitless resource trove and an endless dump, such that the costs of disposal are rarely embedded within the formula of creation, distribution, and consumption. Thus, the idea of disposal—or what happens as a result of your combustion engine creating additional carbon to be "free released" into the atmosphere—is never critically examined, let alone considered for policy change. We say "free released" in scare quotes because we are now witnessing that the devastation of this logic very clearly shows that there is nothing free about this approach to the biosphere. And yet, in one of the few places where this type of progressive, mind-clearing conversation is necessary, it is already off the table due to the imperatives of the

FIGURE 6.1   Sign Greeting Attendees of the Marketplace of the Future, 2019

Source: Authors' image.

events themselves. Again, here we suggest that the true aims of these events as pedagogical episodes might expand the conversations among the global public to not only knowing about the state of the world and the many problems within it, but to beginning to ask really big questions that suggest major changes that will be required in the reckoning with Earth that our species, humans, have only begun to witness.

References

Chazal, N., & Pocrnic, A. (2016). Kony 2012: Intervention narratives and the saviour subject. *International Journal for Crime, Justice and Social Democracy*, *5*(1), 98–112. doi:10.5204/ijcjsd.v5i1.216

Chouliaraki, L. (2006). *The spectatorship of suffering*. SAGE.

Dayan, D., & Katz, E. (1992). *Media events: The live broadcasting of history*. Harvard University Press.

Fiorillo, V. (2020, July 10). Live Aid in Philly: An oral history. *Philadelphia Magazine*. https://www.phillymag.com/news/2020/07/10/live-aid-history/

Kiner, D. (2020, July 13). Live Aid 1985 was literally a life-saving concert for one man 35 years ago. *PennLive Patriot News*. https://www.pennlive.com/life/2020/07/live-aid-1985-was-literally-a-life-saving-concert-for-one-man-35-years-ago.html

Oxfam (2022, January). Inequality kills: The unparalleled action needed to combat unprecedented inequality in the wake of COVID-19. https://oxfamilibrary.openrepository.com/bitstream/handle/10546/621341/bp-inequality-kills-170122-summ-en.pdf

Tester, K. (2001). *Compassion, morality and the media* (1st ed.). Open University Press.

WHO Coronavirus Dashboard. (July 19, 2022). https://covid19.who.int/

WHYY Staff. (2021, May 17). What you need to know about the desecration of MOVE bombing victims' remains. *WHYY*. https://whyy.org/articles/what-you-need-to-know-about-the-desecration-of-move-bombing-victims-remains/

INDEX

Page numbers in *italics* refer to figures.

For Product Safety Concerns and Information please contact our EU
representative GPSR@taylorandfrancis.com
Taylor & Francis Verlag GmbH, Kaufingerstraße 24, 80331 München, Germany